Sc

Scottish Kitchens

To Helen,

Happy cooking!

Best wishes,

Alison

Secrets of the Great Scottish Kitchens

An original selection of recipes from Scotland's finest chefs

compiled by

Alison Jones

Alison Jones
c/o 43–45 Annandale Street, Edinburgh EH7 4AZ

First published by Alison Jones 1994

ISBN 0-9524879-0-X

Front cover photograph, Chef and waiter relaxing in the Strathearn Restaurant, reproduced courtesy of The Gleneagles Hotel

Illustrations © John Beaumont, John Beaumont Illustration Services, 60 Baswich Crest, Stafford ST17 0HJ
except for Greywalls illustration, p*107*, by Wayne Moran

Conversion tables (p*xii*) reproduced by kind permission of Larousse plc, 43–45 Annandale Street, Edinburgh EH7 4AZ

Typeset by Hewer Text Composition Services, Edinburgh
Printed in England by Clays Ltd, St Ives plc

Preface

This has been an enormously exciting book to put together, if a little daunting at times. It contains the accumulated wisdom of some of the very best of Scotland's chefs, with recipes ranging from the traditional to the most modern and imaginative, using to the full the enormous natural resources of Scotland. Salmon, venison and game, the great staples of Scottish country life, feature in these pages of course, often in imaginative and unexpected new interpretations. Alongside them are more unusual ingredients—gulls' eggs, carrageen, junipers, lemon grass, squid ink and so on—reflecting the dynamic and progressive mood of today's restaurateur in Scotland.

This enthusiastic, adventurous mood is especially appropriate for this book, which has been produced to raise funds for Raleigh International. Operation Raleigh, named after the great adventurer Sir Walter Raleigh, was set up at the suggestion of HRH Prince Charles in 1984, to give young people aged 17 to 25 a taste of real adventure and a worthwhile purpose carrying out a variety of environmental and community projects on a ship-based expedition. The original idea was for a limited number of expeditions, but Operation Raleigh grew as more young people discovered its challenge, more scientific projects began to clamour for the aid of Venturers, and expeditions were increasingly welcomed into the most remote and uncharted areas of the world. In 1992 the organization became Raleigh International, reflecting its new, more permanent status, and also its more international composition; each three-month expedition now includes Venturers from the host country and from around the world.

After a selection weekend in Glasgow in May 1994, which involved little food, less sleep and a variety of mind-bending and sinew-stretching challenges, I was accepted for expedition, and will travel to Chile in October 1995 subject to meeting my fund-raising target of £2,950. To all of you who have bought this book, thank you for making my part in this expedition possible. In Chile I am likely to be involved in charting routes above the snow-line in the Andes, rebuilding villages damaged by earthquakes, investigating archaeological sites in the Chonos archipelago, and cataloguing fauna in the area; the exact projects will not be finalized with the Chilean government until nearer the time.

If you would like more details about Raleigh International, send a SAE to Raleigh House, 27 Parsons Green Lane, London SW6 4HZ, or telephone 071-371 8585. And now that you have supported my fundraising by buying this book, I would be delighted to let you know how my expedition to Chile goes! If you want to be kept informed, please write (enclosing an SAE if you can) to Alison Jones, c/o 43–45 Annandale Street, Edinburgh EH7 4AZ.

Acknowledgements

So many people have given me advice, encouragement, and help with this book, and I am very grateful to all of them. Larousse plc, my employers, very generously lent me the benefit of computer equipment and wise professional advice, without both of which I would have floundered! I would particularly like to thank Min Lee and the Production department for their patient expertise, and my colleagues in the editorial department for their enthusiasm and suggestions.

Many thanks to John Beaumont, of John Beaumont Illustration Services, who has cheerfully provided the marvellous artwork developed from drawings sent to me by the chefs; I hope the book brings you many commissions, John!

Thanks too to all the restaurants who have contributed to the book, for allowing me access to your most prized recipes and professional secrets, and also for your encouragement.

Finally, thanks to Beryl, my mum, and Michael for your love and support; I could never have done it without you.

Index of Restaurants

Cromlix House
Kinbuck, Dunblane
Perthshire FK15 9JT
Tel: 0786 822125
(Potato and Cheese Terrine *15*, Baked Salmon with a Horseradish Crust *33*, Lemon Tarte *108*)

The Cross
Tweed Mill Brae
Kingussie PH21 1TC
Tel: 0540 661166
(Raspberry Shortbread with a Passionfruit Coulis *105*)

Cuilmore Cottage
Kinloch Rannoch, by Pitlochry
Perthshire PH16 5QB
Tel: 0882 632218
(Raspberry Pecan Tart *102*)

Dryburgh Abbey Hotel
St Boswells
Roxburghshire TD6 0RQ
Tel: 0835 822261
(Stuffed Avocado with Lime Dressing *11*, Chocolate and Liqueur Pear Cream *112*)

Dunain Park Hotel
Inverness IV3 6JN
Tel: 0463 230512
(Salmon or Sea Bass Baked in a Crust *31*, Basic Sabayon and Variations *32*, Andrea's Camp-fire Chicken *66*)

Glasgow Hilton International
1 William Street
Glasgow G3 8HT
Tel: 041 204 5555
(Medley of Highland Game with Wild Mushrooms on a Rich Game Jus *75*)

The Gleneagles Hotel
Auchterarder
Perthshire PH3 1NF
Tel: 0764 662231
(Pan-fried Sea Bass with Fennel and Crisp Beetroot *59*, Seared Loin of Perthshire Venison served with Sliced Duckling and Gin Sauce *77*, Clapshott Lamb *84*)

Greywalls
Gullane
East Lothian EH31 2EG
Tel: 0620 842144
(Avocado and Honey Mousse *9*, Shortbread Biscuits Crowned by Seasonal Berries and Blackcurrant Meringue with Vanilla and Butterscotch Sauce *106*)

Isle of Eriska Hotel
Ledaig, Oban
Argyll PA37 1SD
Tel: 0631 72371
(Salmon and Leek Terrine *14*, Paupiette of Sole with a Tomato Sauce *46*)

Killiecrankie Hotel
Killiecrankie, by Pitlochry
Perthshire PH16 5LG
Tel: 0796 473220
(Spicy Bean Gumbo *7*)

Kirroughtree Hotel
Newton Stewart
Wigtownshire DG8 6AN
Tel: 0671 402141
(Pan-Fried West Coast Scallops with Roquette Salad, Vegetable Relish and Beurre Blanc *52*)

Lochgreen House
Monktonhill Road,Southwood
Troon KA10 7EN
Tel: 0292 313343
(Pan-fried Fillet of Salmon with an Orange and Tarragon Butter Sauce *37*)

The Lodge on the Loch
Onich, by Fort William
Inverness-shire PH33 6RY
Tel: 08553 238
(Cream of Glen Uig Smoked Alligator Soup *6*)

Loch Torridon Hotel
Torridon, by Achnasheen
Ross-shire IV22 2EY
Tel: 01445 791296
(Wild Mushroom Tartlets in Sherry and Cream *19*, Spinach Roulade with Cream Cheese and Pine Nuts *30*)

Le Marché Noir
2–4 Eyre Place
Edinburgh EH3 5EP
Tel: 031 558 1608
(Leek and Onion Tarte *20*, Wood Pigeon with Honey and Chestnut Sauce *67*, Duo of Poached Pear in Red and White Wine *100*)

Minmore House
Glenlivet
Banffshire AB37 9DB
Tel: 0807 590378
(Raspberry and Almond Pavlova Roulade *101*)

Moat House International
Congress Road
Glasgow G3 8QT
Tel: 041 204 0733
(Nage of Langoustines and Scallops flavoured with Cardamom and Asparagus Tips *50*)

The Murrayshall
Scone
Perthshire PH2 7PH
Tel: 0738 551171
(Mousse of Garden Vegetables and Chicken *12*)

Norton House Hotel
Ingliston
Edinburgh EH28 8LX
Tel: 031 333 1275
(Roast Fillet of Scottish Salmon with Tomato and Pesto Butter *41*)

One Devonshire Gardens
Glasgow G12 0UX
Tel: 041 339 2001
(Cappuccino Brulée *99*)

Ostlers Close
25 Bonnygate, Cupar
Fife KY15 4BU
Tel: 0334 655574
(Fillets of Monkfish in a Light Cheese Herb Batter on a Pesto-flavoured Sauce *57*)

Parklands Hotel and Restaurant
St Leonard's Bank
Perth PH2 8EB
Tel: 0738 622451
(Roulade of Sole and Fresh Langoustine lined with Scottish Smoked Salmon with a light Lemon Butter Sauce *47*)

The Peat Inn
Peat Inn, Cupar
Fife KY15 5LH
Tel: 033484 206
(Pan-fried Venison Liver and Kidney with a Lentil Salad *21*)

La Potinière
Main Street
Gullane EH31 2AA
Tel: 0620 843214
(Leek Pies *24*)

Sheraton Grand Hotel
1 Festival Square
Edinburgh EH3 9SR
Tel: 031 229 9131
(Ayrshire Spring Lamb with Stovies *80*)

Shieldhilll
Quothquan
Biggar ML12 6NA
Tel: 0899 20035
(Fillet of Angus Beef Resting on a Potato Rosti with a Cannelloni of Leek and Haggis *86*, Clafoutis of Apples, Drambuie Ice Cream and Raspberry Coulis *115*)

Sunlaws House Hotel
Kelso
Roxburghshire TD5 8JZ
Tel: 0573 450331
(Roast Breast of Wood Pigeon with Girolles and Foie Gras *68*)

Thainstone House Hotel
Inverurie
Aberdeenshire AB51 5NT
Tel: 0467 621643
(Roulade of Smoked Salmon, Langoustine and Seaweed with Lemon Grass Sauce garnished with a Creel Cage *39*, Roast Loin of Scotch Lamb with Wild Mushroom Tarragon Mousse on a Rosti Potato with Rosemary Sauce *82*)

Three Chimneys Restaurant
Colbost, Dunvegan
Isle of Skye IV55 8ZT
Tel: 01470 511258
(Crab Tart with Lemon Butter Sauce *55*)

Tiroran House
Tiroran
Isle of Mull PA69 6ES
Tel: 06815 232
(Gulls Eggs with Watercress Mayonnaise *17*, Carrageen Jelly with Fresh Raspberries *97*)

Turnberry Hotel
Golf Courses and Spa,
Turnberry
Ayrshire KA26 9LT
Tel: 0655 31000
(Fillets of Rainbow Trout and Scampi with a Sauterne, Tomato and Chervil Cream Sauce *61*)

The Ubiquitous Chip
12 Ashton Lane
Glasgow G12 8SJ
Tel: 041 334 5007
(Caledonian Ice Cream *110*)

Valvona & Crolla
19 Elm Row
Edinburgh EH7 4AA
Tel: 031 556 6066
(Egg Tagliatelli with Wild Mushroom Sauce *64*)

Vintners Rooms
The Vaults
87 Giles Street, Leith
Edinburgh EH6 6BZ
Tel: 031 554 6767
(Bramble and Almond Tart *109*)

Conversion Tables

The majority of recipes in this book use imperial measurements only; a few use both metric and imperial and a very few only metric. I have avoided the temptation to convert all these measurements to both imperial and metric because the conversions we generally work with are not precise; the form in which the recipes are given is the form in which I received them from the chefs, and therefore the only form in which they are guaranteed to produce perfect results! Since many of us use one or the other in the kitchen at home, I include here a guide to metric/imperial conversions, reproduced from the *Chambers Book of Facts* courtesy of Larousse plc.

UK fluid ounces	litres	US fluid ounces	litres	litres	UK fluid ounces	US fluid ounces
1	0.0284	1	0.0296	1	35.2	33.8
2	0.0568	2	0.0592	2	70.4	67.6
3	0.0852	3	0.0888	3	105.6	101.4
4	0.114	4	0.118	4	140.8	135.3
5	0.142	5	0.148	5	176.0	169.1
6	0.170	6	0.178	6	211.2	202.9
7	0.199	7	0.207	7	246.4	236.7
8	0.227	8	0.237	8	281.6	270.5
9	0.256	9	0.266	9	316.8	304.3
10	0.284	10	0.296	10	352.0	338.1
11	0.312	11	0.326	11	387.2	372.0
12	0.341	12	0.355	12	422.4	405.8
13	0.369	13	0.385	13	457.5	439.6
14	0.397	14	0.414	14	492.7	473.4
15	0.426	15	0.444	15	527.9	507.2
20	0.568	20	0.592	20	703.9	676.3
50	1.42	50	1.48	50	1 759.8	1 690.7
100	2.84	100	2.96	100	3 519.6	3 381.5

UK pints	litres
1	0.57
2	1.14
3	1.70
4	2.27
5	2.84
6	3.41
7	3.98
8	4.55
9	5.11
10	5.68
11	6.25
12	6.82
13	7.38
14	7.95
15	8.52
20	11.36

US pints	litres
1	0.47
2	0.95
3	1.42
4	1.89
5	2.37
6	2.84
7	3.31
8	3.78
9	4.26
10	4.73
11	5.20
12	5.68
13	6.15
14	6.62
15	7.10
20	9.46

litres	UK pints	US pints
1	1.76	2.11
2	3.52	4.23
3	5.28	6.34
4	7.04	8.45
5	8.80	10.57
6	10.56	12.68
7	12.32	14.79
8	14.08	16.91
9	15.84	19.02
10	17.60	21.13
11	19.36	23.25
12	21.12	25.36
13	22.88	27.47
14	24.64	29.59
15	26.40	31.70
20	35.20	105.67

ounces	grams
1	28.3
2	56.7
3	85
4	113.4
5	141.7
6	170.1
7	198.4
8	226.8
9	255.1
10	283.5
11	311.7
12	340.2
13	368.5
14	396.9
15	425.2
16	453.6

grams	ounces
1	0.04
2	0.07
3	0.11
4	0.14
5	0.18
6	0.21
7	0.25
8	0.28
9	0.32
10	0.35
20	0.71
30	1.06
40	1.41
50	1.76
60	2.12
70	2.47
80	2.82
90	3.18
100	3.53

pounds	kilograms
1	0.45
2	0.91
3	1.36
4	1.81
5	2.27
6	2.72
7	3.18
8	3.63
9	4.08
10	4.54
11	4.99
12	5.44
13	5.90
14	6.35
15	6.80
16	7.26
17	7.71
18	8.16
19	8.62
20	9.07

kilograms	pounds
1	2.2
2	4.4
3	6.6
4	8.8
5	11
6	13.2
7	15.4
8	17.6
9	19.8
10	22
11	24.3
12	26.5
13	28.7
14	30.9
15	33.1
16	35.3
17	37.5
18	39.7
19	41.9
20	44.1

Soups, Starters and Salads

Braeval

Carrot, Honey and Ginger Soup

created by
NICK NAIRN

Always make this soup in advance, when you have time, and either freeze (I make large quantities to freeze and use as I need it) or chill before use. If you have one, a food processor is best to slice the carrots. After puréeing the soup, pour it into large jugs and plunge them immediately into a sink of very cold water to cool the soup as quickly as possible—this preserves its freshness and colour.

Serves 4

6 oz onions, thinly sliced
small piece root ginger, bruised
3 oz butter
1 tbsp honey
1 lb carrots, scrubbed and finely grated
salt and freshly ground white pepper
squeeze of lemon

Sweat the finely sliced onions and ginger in the butter for 10 minutes—do not brown. Stir in the honey, let it melt, and then add the carrots. Stir to coat the carrots, and pour in enough **boiling** water to cover. Add a little seasoning, and bring back to the boil on a high heat.

Simmer for 45 minutes—until the vegetables are tender. Pour into a liquidizer and process to a purée. Finally check the seasoning, add the lemon juice, and serve with a blob of cream.

Cameron House Hotel and Country Estate

Melon and Scampi Soup

created by
JEFF BLAND

For an extra-special occasion, champagne can be used in place of the cider. Alternatively, for a more economical meal, replace the caviar and salmon eggs with seasonal berries. At Cameron House we use West-Coast scampi, fresh from the Kyle of Lochalsh.

Serves 4

1 melon (Ogen or Charentais)
1 glass dry cider
1 glass Sauternes
1 lemon, segmented
1 lime, segmented
juice of 1 pink grapefruit
12 pieces fresh scampi
¼ oz caviar
¼ oz salmon eggs
chervil leaves

Using a small Parisienne cutter, ball out the melon. Place the balls into 4 soup bowls. Liquidize the remaining melon with the dry cider, wine, lemon, lime and grapefruit juice, reserving a few lemon and lime segments for garnish. Pour over the melon balls. Pan-fry the scampi and place into the soup bowls, and garnish with the caviar, salmon eggs, reserved lemon and lime, and chervil leaves.

Creel Restaurant and Rooms

Smoked Fish Soup

created by

ALAN CRAIGIE

A drive south from Kirkwall across the Churchill barriers to South Ronaldsay will take you to the harbour village of St Margaret's Hope, and one of the most renowned seafood restaurants in Scotland.

Serves 4

- 6 oz onions, sliced
- 4 oz leeks, chopped
- 1 oz butter
- 1 oz plain flour
- 1½ pt fish stock
- 4 oz potato, sliced
- 1 oz parsley, chopped
- 1 lb smoked haddock
- ¼ pt double cream

Sweat the onions and leeks in the butter, then add the flour and cook for a few minutes. Blend in the fish stock a little at a time, and add the raw sliced potato and parsley. Simmer for about half an hour. Cut the haddock into chunks, add to the soup and simmer for a further 10 minutes. To serve season and finish each bowl with a swirl of double cream.

Cream of Glen Uig Smoked Alligator Soup

created by

DAVID WILSON

Alligator may not sound like a Scottish delicacy, but we think that Scotland is in fact the only place in the world that has succeeded in smoking the alligator. In 1991, when Simon Macdonald of Glen Uig perfected the method, the Lodge On The Loch was one of the first to try this new experience, shortly afterwards developing this unique 'Taste of Scotland' soup—the only hotel in the world to make smoked alligator soup at that time and probably still to this day.

Serves 20

- 12 oz button mushrooms, sliced
- 12 oz onion, chopped
- 12 oz white leek, sliced
- ¾ of a bottle of dry white wine
- 8 pt chicken stock
- 8 oz unsalted butter
- 8 oz white flour
- 4 oz smoked Glen Uig alligator
- 1 pt double cream

Sauté the sliced mushrooms, onion and white leek until they just start to colour. Add the white wine and reduce the liquid, add the chicken stock and reduce by a quarter. Meanwhile make a roux by melting the butter and stirring in the flour. Cook for a minute then add the chicken stock mix slowly. Bring to the boil and simmer for 20 minutes. Sieve the soup and discard the leek and mushroom etc. Finely chop the smoked alligator and add to the soup, bring back to the boil, then add the cream. Season and serve, sprinkled with finely chopped herbs (parsley, basil, chives and coriander).

Killiecrankie Hotel

Spicy Bean Gumbo

created by
JOHN RAMSAY

When travelling in the USA, one of my favourite meals was any of the chowder and gumbo soups available. Of course a good Scotch broth is our equivalent, but unfortunately this dish has been ruined by the advent of tins and packet soups and many people are put off by this. So it was my intention to create a hearty, filling soup, appealing to modern tastes but still clinging to the original idea. A bowl of this soup with crusty bread is a meal in itself and a very appealing sight on a cold wintry day. By using vegetable stock and adding less liquid this can be made into a vegetarian stew, jazzed up with the addition of pistachios, mushrooms or anything at all you want!

Serves lots

- 2 lb mixed beans (black-eye, flageolet, haricot etc—any mixture)
- 2 large onions
- 1 lb carrots
- 1 lb celery
- 2–3 fresh chillies (or 4 tsp chilli powder)
- 1 tbsp whole cumin seeds
- 2–3 bay leaves
- 2 tins plum tomatoes, chopped
- 2 pt white stock (ham or good veg preferably)
- 1 pt lager
- 4 tbsp tomato purée
- 1 tsp cocoa powder
- seasoning

Soak the beans overnight in plenty of cold water. Dice the onion, carrots and celery and sauté in olive oil with the finely diced chillies. Add the cumin seeds and bay leaves, stirring over a high heat until the cumin is well warmed. Add the tomatoes and beans, mixing well, then add the stock and lager and bring to the boil. Finally, add the tomato purée and cocoa powder and simmer until all the vegetables and beans are cooked. Check seasoning and enjoy!

Cameron House Hotel and Country Estate

Lanark Blue Cheese Mousse with Salad Leaves and Hazelnut Dressing

created by

JEFF BLAND

The blue cheese takes over the flavour so beautifully that it is impossible to tell that this is really a chicken mousse. Without the cheese, the mousse is ideal for use in terrines.

Serves 4

for the blue cheese mousse:

- ½ lb minced chicken
- 2 oz Lanark blue cheese, grated
- 1 egg white
- ½ pt double cream
- seasoning

for the salad and hazelnut dressing:

- 1 egg yolk
- 2 fl oz walnut oil
- 2 fl oz olive oil
- 2 fl oz white wine
- 1 fl oz white wine vinegar
- seasoning
- 1 oz hazelnuts, crushed
- 1 oz walnuts, broken
- mixed salad leaves (eg radiccio, frizzy, etc)

Mix the chicken, Lanark blue cheese, egg white, cream and seasoning over ice until smooth or in a food processor with a few ice cubes. Pipe into a buttered dariole mould or small cup then smooth over the top. Cook in a warm oven in a bain-marie, or in a saucepan in a water bath, for 20–25 minutes. Meanwhile prepare the hazelnut dressing; place the egg yolk into a small mixing bowl and add both oils, whisking slowly, and gradually add the white wine, vinegar, seasoning and nuts.

Turn out the mousse and glaze with hollandaise sauce. Place the mousse in the centre of a serving plate and surround with a selection of salad leaves. Surround the leaves with the hazelnut dressing and garnish with small balls of Lanark blue cheese and slices of truffle.

Avocado and Honey Mousse

created by
PAUL BARON

Serves 4

2 avocados
juice of 3 lemons
3 tbsp honey (clear is best)
3 leaves gelatine
½ pt mayonnaise
½ pt double cream

Blend the avocados, lemon juice and honey until smooth, and pass the mixture through a fine sieve. Dissolve the gelatine in water then heat slowly in a pan. Place the mayonnaise in a bowl and fold in the avocado mix. Add the gelatine to the mixture and season to taste with salt and ground white pepper. Finally, whip the double cream to the ribbon stage and lightly fold into the mixture. Leave to rest in the refrigerator for about 6 hours before use. Use within 2–3 days.

Grilled Goats Cheese, Courgette, Red Pepper and Plum Tomato

created by

ANDREW RADFORD

Wine suggestion: Vouvray, Clos du Bourg 1982, demi-sec (Société Huet)

Serves 4

- 2 red peppers
- 4 goats cheeses
- 4 small courgettes
- 4 plum tomatoes
- 4 slices brioche
- 4 oz pesto
- olive oil
- salt and pepper
- 2 oz basil and parsley

Roast the peppers, remove their skins and quarter them lengthways. Cut the brioche slices into rings or squares the same size or slightly larger than the goats cheeses. Cut the tomatoes in half lengthways, and do the same with the courgettes. Grill the courgettes, peppers and plum tomatoes, and then the goats cheeses and brioche.

To assemble the dish, place a brioche topped with cheese in the centre of each serving plate and haphazardly arrange the pepper, tomato and courgette around. Mould the pesto into nuggets between dessertspoons and place one on each dish. Sprinkle with the chopped basil and parsley, dribble olive oil over, and serve.

Dryburgh Abbey Hotel

Stuffed Avocado with Lime Dressing

created by
PATRICK RUSE

This is a very easy, very luxurious vegetarian starter, ideal as the first course for a summer dinner party.

Serves 4

2 large avocados
2 oz fresh asparagus
3 oz cooked wholemeal rice
3 oz cashew nuts
1 spring onion, chopped
2 oz pineapple, diced
2 fl oz natural yoghurt
1 oz hazelnuts
1 tbsp raisins, soaked in 2 tbsp brandy

for the lime dressing:
zest and juice of 2 small limes
8 oz crème fraîche
1 tbsp chives, finely chopped

For the dressing, blanch the lime zest in boiling water for 2 minutes, then mix all the dressing ingredients together. Halve and skin the avocados, and remove the stones. Combine all the remaining ingredients together and arrange in the avocado halves. To serve, either coat each avocado with a little dressing or serve the dressing separately. Garnish as desired.

The Murrayshall

Mousse of Garden Vegetables and Chicken

created by
ANDY CAMPBELL

Serves 28 (2 terrines)

6 large chicken suprêmes
3 egg whites
¼ pt double cream
3 lb smoked back bacon
8 large carrots, cut into large batons and blanched
2 lb fine green beans, blanched
1 red, green and yellow peppers, skin removed
½ oz soft green peppercorns
chives, parsley and tarragon, chopped and marinated in Madeira

for the sauce:

2 oranges
1 pt orange juice
1 oz chives
4 oz fresh coriander
1 pt plain yoghurt

First make the sauce. Cut the orange rind into julienne and cook in the orange juice. Place all the sauce ingredients except the yoghurt together in a pan and reduce by half, then stir in the yoghurt when cold.

Robot Coupe the suprêmes of chicken with the egg whites to give a smooth mousse; place the mixture in a bowl over ice to chill. Gradually add the cream, mixing slowly (it is important not to overbeat). Line two terrines with back bacon, leaving the ends overhanging to form a lid later. Pour half the prepared mousse into the lined terrines. Place the carrot batons on top of the mousse, leaving space between each baton. Pour on another covering of mousse. Alternate the garden vegetables with the mousse until the top of the terrine is reached, then overlap the bacon to encase the mousse, cover with foil, and replace the terrine lids. Cook slowly in a bain-marie on the bottom shelf of the oven (Gas 3/325°F/160°C) for 1–1½ hours. Check after 45 minutes, to ensure that the water has not boiled away, and keep checking every 15 minutes or so.

When cooked, keep the terrines chilled in the refrigerator ready for use. To serve, pour the sauce onto a serving plate and place a slice of terrine on top. Garnish with 5 small bundles of dried cucumber with a sprig of coriander placed neatly on top. Chill, then present to awed guests.

Salmon and Leek Terrine

created by
ALAN CLARK

In this unusual starter the heat of the leeks cooks the salmon delicately. It is perfect served in a summery meal sliced and garnished with a raspberry vinaigrette.

8½ oz salmon fillet
8 medium leeks
24 baby leeks
salt and freshly ground black pepper

Cut the salmon and trimmed leeks to the length of a terrine dish. Line the terrine dish with cling film, leaving an overlap. Then place the leeks in a pan of boiling water to cook for 4 minutes before adding the baby leeks for a further 3 minutes. Remove from the heat, drain, and place a layer of large leeks on the base of the terrine. Lay a layer of salmon on top of the hot leeks, add one large leek on either side, and lay the baby leeks on the top. Repeat this layering process, seasoning as required. Finally, wrap the cling film tightly round the terrine, press, and place in the refrigerator to chill.

Potato and Cheese Terrine

created by
STEPHEN ROBERTSON

This recipe is easily prepared in the home. It makes an impressive starter served with green grapes, French leaves and vinaigrette, or try it as a lunch or supper dish, served with a more substantial mixed salad and a fruity vinaigrette.

Serves 6–8

5 large potatoes, peeled
2 lb assorted cheeses (eg Lanark Blue, Orkney Smoked, Cheddar and Gruyère)
2 oz chopped mixed herbs
3 egg yolks
2 oz onions, finely chopped
pinch seasoning

Thinly slice the potatoes and blanch them in boiling water for 5 minutes. Line a 1 lb loaf tin with cling film and then arrange a layer of potato slices over the bottom. Grate the cheeses and mix in the chopped herbs, egg yolks, chopped onion and seasoning, then spoon about a quarter of this mixture over the potatoes. Add another layer of potato slices, and continue layering in this way until the tin is full. Cover the tin with tin foil and place it in a deep roasting tray. Half-fill the tray with boiling water, then place in a moderate oven for 30 minutes.

After removing the tray from the oven, place a weight firmly on top of the loaf tin and leave to cool. When it is just warm, place in the refrigerator to chill completely for 3–4 hours.

When ready to serve, remove the terrine from the cling film and slice. Coat each slice with flour and pan fry in a little oil and butter until golden brown.

Ballachulish Hotel

Highland Game and Chantrelle Mushroom Terrine

created by

KENNY MICHIE

This 'Taste of Scotland' dish is the perfect entrée to many of our Highland dinners. Its combination of duck and game flavours married with delicate chantrelle mushrooms is a firm favourite with our guests.

½ lb chantrelle mushrooms
6 oz mallard breast
2 lb game trimmings
4 egg whites
1 pt double cream
1 lb smoked back bacon

Sauté the chantrelle mushrooms in clarified butter for a minute then strain off the excess butter. Cut the duck breasts into strips and sauté as above. Place the game trimmings in a food processor and mix, then slowly add the egg whites, one at a time, and then equally slowly add the cream, mixing all the time. Season with salt and pepper.

Line a terrine dish with smoked bacon, and layer the processed game, mushrooms and strips of duck on top of the bacon. Fold the bacon over the top and cover with cling film, then place a lid on top to press. Cook in a bain-marie (or in a container placed in a pan of water over heat) for 45 minutes. Cool, slice, and serve with Cumberland sauce.

Gulls Eggs with Watercress Mayonnaise

created by
SUE BLOCKEY

The season is short, but gulls' eggs are delicious. On Mull we gather them from rocky islets close by the hotel. The ideal date is about the 9th May; if on that date we find a nest with only one or two eggs, we take those and the gulls automatically lay more eggs. However, if there are three eggs in a nest we leave them, as they will already have started to form chicks. The same numbers of gulls nest year after year on the skerries, and taking a few eggs at the beginning of the season makes no difference to their breeding habits. We are always careful not to disturb the nest or surroundings in any way.

1 or 2 gulls' eggs per person

for the mayonnaise:

2 eggs
salt and pepper to taste
pinch curry powder
small clove garlic
tbsp vinegar
good quality olive oil
small bunch watercress

Boil the gulls' eggs carefully for 15 minutes. Remove from the water and tap both ends smartly to crack the shell. Leave in cold water. Leave the shells on to serve, as they look so pretty. I serve them in individual wicker baskets with a little pot of mayonnaise.

Meanwhile prepare the mayonnaise. Put all the ingredients except the olive oil and watercress in a blender and with the power on slowly dribble in the olive oil until you have a good thick mayonnaise texture. A nice variation is to reduce a tablespoon of dry martini with a thin slice of onion and a very little marmite, just the tip of a teaspoon, then pour into the blender for a final whizz. Put the mayonnaise into individual pots each decorated with a sprig of watercress and serve with the gulls' eggs.

Loch Torridon Hotel

Wild Mushroom Tartlets in Sherry and Cream

created by

GERALDINE GREGORY

Our guests have great fun collecting and identifying the many different varieties of mushrooms from our woods.

Serves 4

4 × shortcrust pastry cases, 6″ × 3″
12 oz wild mushrooms
clove of garlic, chopped
2 tbsp dry sherry
5 fl oz single cream
salt, black pepper and nutmeg

for the salad leaves and walnut oil vinaigrette:

mixed lettuce leaves
2 tbsp walnut oil
1 tbsp white wine vinegar
seasoning
freshly chopped parsley

Bake blind 4 shortcrust pastry cases. Meanwhile sauté the wild mushrooms in a little butter with the garlic, then add the dry sherry and reduce. Add the single cream and reduce further, then season with salt and black pepper with a pinch of nutmeg. Fill the warm tartlets with the mushroom mixture and serve on mixed lettuce leaves which have been tossed in the vinaigrette, and sprinkle with parsley.

Leek and Onion Tarte

created by
NEIL ROSS

Serves 4

for the shortcrust pastry:
- 5 oz plain flour
- 2 oz butter
- 3 tbsp cream

for the filling:
- 2 whole leeks, diced small
- 2 oz onions, finely chopped
- 2 oz butter
- 4 eggs
- ½ pt cream
- salt and pepper

To make the shortcrust pastry, rub in together the flour and butter, add the cream and blend until the mixture comes together. Allow to stand in the refrigerator for 20 minutes.

Lightly sauté the leeks and chopped onions in a little butter then leave to cool. Meanwhile mix together the eggs and cream and season.

After the pastry has rested, roll it out thinly and line individual greased tarte tins. Bake the tarte cases blind for about 10 minutes at Gas 3/325°F/170°C. Place the leek and onion mixture into the tarte cases and pour the eggs and cream mixture on top. Bake for a further 10 minutes. Garnish with salad leaves and serve.

Pan-fried Venison Liver and Kidney with a Lentil Salad

created by

DAVID WILSON

Venison liver and kidney may prove difficult to procure as quite often the livers are retained by the 'guns' and the kidneys discarded. Both are well worth seeking out as they are extremely tender with a delicious, delicate flavour. If you cannot get access to wild venison, try one of the venison farms.

Serves 4 as a starter

for the sauce:

1 tbsp chopped shallots
4 fl oz (150ml) red wine
1 oz (30g) caster sugar
1 tbsp sherry vinegar
8 fl oz (250ml) brown stock
1 oz (30g) unsalted butter, chilled

8 oz (225g) brown lentils
½ small onion, studded with a clove
1 bay leaf
2 tbsp chopped shallots
salt and pepper
12 oz (350g) venison liver
2 venison kidneys
mixed green salad leaves
vinaigrette dressing

Begin with the sauce, which can be made in advance. Put the chopped shallots in a pan with a film of vegetable oil, sauté until translucent, then add the red wine, sugar and sherry vinegar. Reduce until caramelized. Then add the brown stock, stir to amalgamate all the ingredients, and allow to reduce by about a third. Dice the chilled butter and whisk it into the sauce. Season. (Sauce-making is an art, and it may be necessary to adjust quantities to get the consistency and flavours you want; much depends on the quality of the stock.)

To cook the lentils, put them in a pan and cover with cold water, add the ½ onion and the bay leaf and bring to the boil. Simmer gently until cooked; do not let them become mushy, they should still have a 'bite'. Remove the onion and bay leaf and keep the lentils warm. Put a film of vegetable oil in a sauté pan and sauté the chopped shallots until translucent, then add to lentils. Season the lentils with salt and freshly ground black pepper.

To cook the liver and kidneys, slice them thinly and season with salt and freshly ground black pepper. Put a film of vegetable oil in a large sauté pan and heat until the oil begins to smoke, then place the slices of liver and kidney in the pan. Cook for 30 seconds then turn over for a further 45 seconds (the cooking time depends on personal preference and the thickness of the slices, but ideally the meat should be pink in the centre).

To serve toss the salad leaves in the vinaigrette dressing and arrange them around a plate. Spoon the lentils into the centre, place the liver and kidneys on top and spoon the sauce over. Serve immediately.

Champany Inn

Mushrooms à la Greque

created by

E A DAVIDSON

As we feature Aberdeen Angus beef and Shetland salmon cooked over a charcoal grill at Champany, it is difficult to give a typical recipe that would translate to a domestic kitchen. However, this is a simple but delicious salad dish that we serve regularly, and so many of our customers beg for the recipe.

3 lb button mushrooms
1 pt water
4 fl oz oil
2 fl oz lemon juice
10 coriander seeds
10 peppercorns
sprig of parsley
bay leaf
salt to taste

Simmer all the ingredients together for 10 minutes. Do not strain, but allow to cool and serve in the cooling liquid.

Leek Pies (Pithiviers de Poireaux)

created by
HILARY BROWN

These little pies are filled with a purée of leeks and are served surrounded by a fresh herb sauce. Large ones can be served as a starter or vegetarian main course (in which case omit the stock in the sauce) or smaller ones as an accompaniment to slices of lamb fillet.

Serves 4

- 12 oz (350g) flaky pastry (see below)
- 1 egg yolk
- seasoning

for the flaky pastry:

- 8¾ oz (250g) plain flour
- 1 tsp salt
- 10½ oz (300g) unsalted butter, at room temperature but still quite hard

for the leek purée:

- 1 lb (45g) white part of leeks
- ½ oz (15g) unsalted butter
- 3 tbsp double cream
- 4–6 leaves mint or basil

for the herb sauce:

- 2 handfuls mixed fresh herbs (tarragon, parsley, mint, chervil)
- 5 fl oz (150ml) chicken stock
- 7½ fl oz (225ml) double cream

To make the flaky pastry, place the flour, salt and 1¾ oz (50g) of the butter in the bowl of your food processor, fitted with the cutting blade, and process until the butter has disappeared and is evenly dispersed throughout the flour. Add just under 5 fl oz (150ml) very cold water and process for 30 seconds or so, or until the dough forms a ball. Do not over-mix.

Turn out on to a lightly floured surface, form into a ball, flatten slightly, then make large cuts in one direction, then at an angle, so that you are forming diamonds. This helps the dough to relax quickly. Place inside a plastic bag and refrigerate for an hour. Meanwhile, place the remaining block of butter on a large piece of cling film, cover with another, then press it very firmly to break it up. Ease it into a shape 6″ (15cm) square, with neat, square corners. If the room is very hot, refrigerate; if not, leave it out until the dough has rested.

Remove the dough from its bag, and place on a lightly floured work surface. Gently tease it into a square shape with square corners and roll it out into a 10″ (20cm) square. Place the butter in the centre, having given it a quarter turn so that the points of the butter are half-way along the edges of the dough, and slightly in from the edge. Fold the corners of the dough in towards the centre of the butter, so that the butter is completely covered. Press down gently with your rolling pin to seal the edges. Brush off any excess flour which may prevent the dough from sticking together.

Keeping the corners as square as possible, roll the dough into a long strip. Lift it now and again to make sure that it is not sticking, and sprinkle the surface with a little more flour. Roll in the one direction, without turning the dough round or over.

Mark the strip into three even lengths, then fold the bottom third, the one nearest you, over the centre section, then lift the top third over the centre. Line them up so that the edges and corners match perfectly, then press the edges together with your rolling pin to seal them. Lift it up, lightly flour the surface again and give the pastry a quarter turn in an anti-clockwise direction, so that the folded edges are now lying on the left and right. Roll out once again, using light but forceful strokes in the one direction only. Fold as before, seal the edges, then carefully place in a large plastic bag. Place on a tray and refrigerate for another half hour.

Repeat this procedure, giving the pastry a quarter turn, folding and sealing twice more, so that the pastry has had all six rollings. Keep covered in the refrigerator until needed.

To make the pies, clean the leeks by splitting in half and rinsing under cold water. Chop them finely by hand or in a food processor (in which case stop before they become too soft). Melt the butter in a pan and let it colour ever so slightly, then add the leeks. Stir occasionally to make sure that they are not sticking. By the end of the cooking time, they should have softened and the mixture should be fairly dry. If still rather moist, turn up the heat and, stirring constantly, let the excess moisture evaporate. Taste and if necessary add another ½ tsp of salt. Turn out on to a plate to cool thoroughly before using.

Lightly flour your work surface. Roll the pastry out to a thickness of just less than ⅛″ (3mm). Using a 4″ (10cm) and a 4½″–5″ (12–13cm) cutter, cut out 4 rounds of each size. You may have to lay the scraps of pastry on top of each other and re-roll to get all 8 rounds. (If making smaller *pithiviers* use 3½″ and 3¾″ (8 and 9cm) cutters.) Moisten the outer surface of the smaller rounds with a little cold water, place a mound of leek filling in the centre and top with a large leaf of fresh mint or basil. Make sure there is a ½″ (1cm) border which is completely leek free, as this is essential if the pastry is going to stick together without any gaps where the filling would come out during the cooking.

Place the larger rounds over the filling, matching outer edges perfectly. Press together well, without damaging the cut edges. Place an upturned cutter, the same circumference as the mound, over it, while you knock up the cut edges with a sharp knife. The upturned cutter ensures that the finish is neat and even, and you don't have to touch the pastry too much. Knock up the edge by making several cuts in the pastry all the way around. This ensures that the pastry is sealed together and that the pastry will rise evenly.

Make a decorative border by pressing your thumb outwards while pushing the edge of a knife in towards the centre. Repeat, at a thumb's breadth apart, all around the *pithiviers.*

Moisten a baking tray with a little cold water, shake off any excess, and place the *pithiviers* on it, leaving ½" (1cm) space at least between each one. Allow to rest in the refrigerator for at least an hour. Preheat oven to Gas 6/400°F/200°C.

Meanwhile, make the sauce by dropping the herbs into lightly salted boiling water. Bring back to the boil, then drain through a sieve. Refresh with plenty of cold running water, to set the colour. Drain, squeeze out most of the moisture and place in your liquidizer (you will get a smoother sauce with a liquidizer rather than a food processor).

Place the stock in a pan, bring to the boil and reduce it a little by fast boiling. Add the cream, bring back to the boil and simmer until it has reduced enough to form a light coating consistency. Pour on to the herbs and blend until a smooth sauce is formed. Pour back into the pan, using a rubber bowl scaper to remove every last drop. Rinse the bowl out with a very little hot water and add to the sauce. Taste for seasoning, adding a little salt if necessary.

Beat the egg yolk with a few drops of cold water, then, using a pastry brush, give each *pithivier* a light coating of egg wash. Be careful not to let it dribble down the sides as this would seal the edges together, thus preventing even rising.

Using a small sharp pointed knife, lightly mark the tops. Do this by marking from the centre a curved line to one of the scallops around the edge. Repeat, starting from the centre again, and curve towards the next scallop, until all the scallops are used up. Bake for 15–20 minutes, until risen, golden brown and crisp.

Reheat the sauce carefully. Do not let it boil for more than 2–3 minutes otherwise the colour will spoil. Check taste and consistency.

Ladle or spoon some sauce on to each warmed serving plate, and swirl the plate carefully to spread it evenly around. Loosen each *pithivier* with a fish slice or spatula and sit one in the centre of each plate. Serve immediately.

Adapted with permission from David and Hilary Brown's *La Poitinière and Friends* (Harmony, Gullane, 1994)

Main Courses

Loch Torridon Hotel

Spinach Roulade with Cream Cheese and Pine Nuts

created by

GERALDINE GREGORY

A luxurious and really stunning vegetarian dish.

2 oz butter
2 oz plain flour
4 eggs, separated
5 fl oz milk, warmed
8 oz freshly cooked and puréed spinach
8 oz cream cheese
4 oz Stilton
5 fl oz single cream
pine nuts to coat

Melt the butter and add the flour to make a roux. Then add the milk and allow to cool slightly before adding the egg yolks and spinach. Whisk the egg whites to full volume and fold into the mixture. Line a 12″ Swiss-roll tin with parchment paper and fill with the mixture; bake for 10–15 minutes at Gas 4/350°F/230°C.

In the meantime, cream the cream cheese with the Stilton and single cream. Spread this mixture over the cooked roulade and roll up carefully. Cut into slices and top with pine nuts. Grill before serving.

Dunain Park Hotel

Salmon or Sea Bass Baked in a Crust

created by
ANN NICOLL

Serves 4–6

3–4 lb (1.5–2 kg) salmon tail on the bone or whole sea bass
mixed herbs (dill, parsley and tarragon)
coarse rock salt

for the paste:
4 oz (125g) coarse rock salt
4 oz (125 g) plain flour
water to mix

to garnish:
fresh mixed herbs

Preheat the oven to Gas 7/425°F/220°C.

Clean and descale the fish and remove fins. Fill the cavity with dill, parsley and tarragon. Place a bed of salt on a baking tin and lay the fish on top. Mix the flour and salt together and add enough water to make a softish paste; if it is too dry and stiff it will not spread over the fish, and if it is too wet and soft it will run off. Spread the paste evenly over the fish. If you wish, mark 'scales' with a spoon to make the finished dish really stunning.

Bake for approximately 20–30 minutes, until the crust has just turned golden. The crust should not be eaten, but to impress your guests you can crack it open at the table; the skin will come away with the crust. Serve hot or cold with hollandaise sauce (see over) or a lemon- and dill-flavoured live yoghurt.

Dunain Park Hotel

Basic Sabayon and Variations

created by

ANN NICOLL

6 egg yolks	¾ lb (350 g) salted butter
2 tbsp water	¾ lb (350 g) unsalted butter

Liquidize the egg yolks and water. Melt the two types of butter in a pan and when melted add to the yolk mixture in the liquidizer one ladleful at a time, keeping the machine running throughout.

Variations

Sorrel Sauce Remove the spines from a handful of sorrel leaves and add the leaves to the basic sauce.

Browned Butter Cook some butter until it is a caramel-brown colour and add to the basic sauce.

Hollandaise Melt a little butter in a pan and fry a chopped shallot. Add tarragon vinegar or white wine vinegar and 6–8 whole peppercorns (do not crush the peppercorns—crushed you get heat, but whole you get flavour). Reduce the sauce and add the strained essence to the basic sabayon.

Mint Bearnaise As for the hollandaise above, but use tarragon vinegar, fresh mint and a dessertspoon of mint jelly.

Cromlix House

Baked Salmon with a Horseradish Crust

created by
STEPHEN ROBERTSON

One of the most attractive and romantic features about Cromlix House is its private chapel, which holds up to forty guests. This elegant dish would be perfect to serve at a truly memorable wedding breakfast.

Serves 4

4 salmon fillets (each 5–6 oz)
lemon juice
melted butter

for the crust:

1 tbsp horseradish
1 tbsp fresh breadcrumbs
1 tsp lemon juice
1 tsp chopped mixed herbs
1 egg yolk
pinch sesame seeds
pinch paprika
seasoning

for the hollandaise:

¼ lb butter
3 egg yolks
juice of 1 lemon
2 tbsp tarragon vinegar
seasoning

Preheat the oven to Gas 6/400°F/200°C.

Trim and season the salmon, then brush the fillets with lemon juice and melted butter. Combine all the crust ingredients, then spread a very thin layer of this paste over the salmon fillets and bake for 10–15 minutes, until just cooked.

Meanwhile, prepare the hollandaise. Melt the butter and place the egg yolks, lemon juice, tarragon vinegar and seasoning into a Robot coupe. Turn the machine on and slowly add the melted butter.

Serve the salmon while still warm with the hollandaise and a crisp green salad.

Scottish Salmon Millefeuille with Watercress Cream

created by
IAN GREEN

This recipe is typical of Caledonian Thistle cuisine; fresh local produce, cooked and presented with flair and imagination.

Chef's tip: semi-freeze the salmon first to make it easier to slice thinly. If your oven is too small to accommodate 12 stacks of filo pastry, make 6 stacks of 4 each, brushed with melted butter to stop them sticking, then gently lever apart when baked.

Serves 4

for the millefeuille:

8 oz filo pastry
2 oz melted butter
1 lb salmon fillet, skinned and thinly sliced
4 oz leek, thinly sliced

for the sauce:

1 bunch watercress
2 oz shallots or onions, chopped
¼ pt white wine
¼ pt whipping or double cream
juice of ½ lemon

Pre-heat oven to Gas 6/400°F/200°C.

Cut the pastry into 24 rectangles, each 4″ × 2″. Lay 12 sheets of pastry on a baking sheet, brush with melted butter, then lay another 12 sheets on top and brush again. Bake until crisp and golden, approximately 5–10 minutes.

Cover 8 of these double sheets with salmon and leeks,

season, and double these 8 up to give 4 stacks. Bake for a further 5–10 minutes, until the salmon is cooked, then cover with the last 4 sheets and keep warm.

Chop half the watercress and cook with the onion in white wine, reduce by half. Add the cream and reduce until thickening, then season with lemon juice. Spoon on to hot serving plates, place the millefeuille on the sauce, and garnish with the remaining watercress.

Steamed Escalopes of Salmon with Elderflower Wine

created by
COLIN DRUMMOND

This delicate dish is delicious served with new potatoes.

Serves 4

- 4 escalopes of salmon, each 5 oz, cut on the slant from a salmon fillet
- 1 glass elderflower wine (commercial elderflower presse will work just as well)
- 1 pt good clear chicken stock
- sprigs of elderflower or flat-leaf parsley to garnish
- 1 oz celery, finely diced
- 2 oz unsalted butter

Preheat oven to medium–hot (Gas 4–5/350–400°F/180–200°C).

Use a large, shallow copper or stainless steel pan, capable of taking the escalopes comfortably. Butter the pan and sprinkle the diced celery over the base. Lay in the escalopes and season, using plenty of freshly ground black pepper. Gently add the elderflower wine and the simmering chicken stock until the liquid barely covers the fish (reserve any excess stock). Cover the dish with a cartouche, a round of buttered greaseproof paper cut to fit the circumference, and place in the oven for 7–10 minutes, or until the salmon is firm to the touch. Remove the escalopes directly onto warm serving plates.

The cooking liquid should now be of a syrupy consistency. Add to it another ladleful of the reserved chicken stock, and bring the sauce to the boil. Knock through the butter to produce the consistency of a thin sauce and pour over the fish. Serve immediately, garnished with sprigs of elderflower or flat-leaf parsley.

Pan-fried Fillet of Salmon with an Orange and Tarragon Butter Sauce with Fresh Sorrel

created by

BILL COSTLEY

To preserve the attractive appearance of the salmon fillets, handle very gently and cook on the presentation side first.

Serves 4

- 4 fillets of salmon, each 6 oz
- 2 oz olive oil
- salt and freshly ground black pepper
- 8 oz sorrel (or spinach)
- 1 oz butter
- 1 small onion, finely chopped
- 16 fresh orange segments
- pinch nutmeg
- blanched orange zest

for the sauce:

- 10 leaves of tarragon
- ½ fl oz champagne vinegar
- ½ fl oz dry vermouth
- 2 fl oz double cream
- 4 oz unsalted butter
- pinch salt and cayenne pepper
- orange juice to taste

Heat the olive oil in a medium sauté pan and gently cook the seasoned salmon fillets on both sides for about 5–10 minutes. Meanwhile, wash and dry the sorrel. Place the butter in a small pan, add the onion and cook for 1 minute without colour, then add the chopped sorrel and cook for a further minute. Season with salt, nutmeg and freshly ground pepper and set aside.

To make the sauce, roughly chop the tarragon and reduce in the vinegar, add the vermouth and further reduce before adding the cream. Then gently add the diced butter whisking continuously over a warm heat (do not boil). Season with salt and cayenne, add the orange juice and pass through a fine sieve.

To serve, pour the warm sauce into the centre of each plate to form a pool, place the salmon fillet on top and garnish with the warm sorrel and onion and the orange segments and zest. Serve immediately.

Thainstone House Hotel and Country Club

Roulade of Smoked Salmon, Langoustine and Seaweed with Lemon Grass Sauce garnished with a Creel Cage

created by

BILL GIBB

Fresh, local produce from one of the finest areas in Scotland is prepared traditionally at Thainstone by Bill Gibb, fresh from a successful expedition to Singapore as part of the Scottish culinary team. Nori seaweed, much used in Japanese cooking, can be bought in dried sheets at specialist food shops.

Serves 4

for the roulade:

- 120g sole
- 4 large langoustines
- 1 egg white
- 150ml cream
- 150g smoked salmon
- 4 sheets of nori seaweed

for the lemon grass sauce:

- 1 yellow pepper
- 25g shallots
- 15g ginger
- 15g lemon grass
- 50ml white wine
- 250ml fish stock
- 250ml cream
- 25g butter
- 25g tomato concasse
- seasoning

to garnish:

- 50g choux pastry
- 6 large prawns
- 12 springs of dill

Prepare the langoustine mousseline; blend the sole and langoustines in a food processor and slowly add the egg white with the blades still turning. Pass through a fine sieve into a bowl over ice, then mix in the cream and chill. Line the smoked salmon with seaweed, spread the mousseline over evenly, season, and roll into four small roulades. Wrap each in cling film.

Using a small piping bag, pipe the choux pastry over four greased diarole moulds, to make creel cages, and bake in a hot oven until golden brown.

Purée the yellow pepper and sweat down in a pan with the shallots, ginger, lemon grass and white wine. Reduce the liquid and add the fish stock. Simmer for 10 minutes then pass into a clean pan and reduce with the cream.

Cook the salmon roulades in fish stock, then remove and allow to rest. Meanwhile clean and split the prawns down the middle, remove the vein, and poach in a little fish stock ready for garnishing. Remove the cling film from the roulades carefully, then slice the roulades and dress on top of choux croûte on four serving plates. Bring the sauce to first boil and finish with the butter and tomato concasse. Pour the sauce around the roulade and decorate with large prawn tails and sprigs of dill. Finish with the creel dish in the centre of each plate.

Norton House Hotel

Roast Fillet of Scottish Salmon with Tomato and Pesto Butter

created by
DAVID BURNS

This recipe for pesto makes a jarful of wonderfully summery paste. If you sprinkle olive oil over the surface and keep it in a preserving jar in the refrigerator it will keep its glorious pungent flavour for several months.

Serves 2

for the pesto:

8 oz pine kernels
3 handfuls fresh basil leaves
⅓ litre (12 fl oz) virgin olive oil
6–8 garlic cloves
4 oz Reggiano parmesan

for the beurre blanc:

3 shallots
1 dsp sherry vinegar
2 dsp double cream
3 oz unsalted butter, cut into small pieces

2 tbsp nut oil
2 skinned salmon fillets, each 6 oz
3 plum tomatoes, peeled and diced

In a food processor, blend together the pine kernels, basil, olive oil and garlic until you have a very fine cream purée (the longer you process the ingredients, the better the final result). Grate the Parmesan finely and add it to the other ingredients, keeping the machine running, until you have a porridge-like consistency.

For the beurre blanc, finely chop the peeled shallots and place in a small saucepan with 2 tbsp cold water and the sherry vinegar. Bring to the boil and cook until all the moisture has evaporated and the shallots are quite dry. Now add the cream, bring back to the boil, and whisk in the butter over a low heat. When all the butter has been incorporated, mix in ⅔ dsp of pesto and season. Keep the sauce warm while you cook the salmon.

Heat the nut oil in a frying pan until very hot, and fry the salmon fillets quickly on both sides for 30 seconds to give a nice colour. Transfer to a lightly greased ovenproof dish, season, and place in a hot oven for 5–6 minutes. Place the sauce onto warm serving plates, sprinkle with the tomato, and place the salmon fillets on top. Serve with a green salad and hot new potatoes.

Baked Cod With Leek and Salsa Gratin

created by
ANDREW RADFORD

Wine suggestion: Wairau River Sauvignon Blanc, from New Zealand

Serves 4

4 cod portions (each 6 oz)
olive oil
salt and pepper
1 lb leek, cut into rings
8 oz new potato rings, cooked
6 oz salsa
4 oz brioche crumbs
butter sauce
chopped chives

To make the butter sauce, melt a knob of butter and add a little white wine, white wine vinegar and chopped shallots. Reduce briefly, then stir in a little cream and some more butter. Keep warm until required.

Place the cod portions on a baking tray, brush with olive oil and season. Grill for 3–4 minutes. Meanwhile pan-fry the potato rings and leek. Spoon a little salsa onto each cod portion, sprinkle with brioche crumbs, and gratinate (brown under a grill).

Spoon some potato and leek rings in the centre of each of 4 serving plates, and place a cod portion on top of each. Pour some butter sauce along the side, sprinkle with chopped chives, and serve.

Ardanaiseig Hotel

Spirals of Sole with Langoustines

created by

SIMON J BAILEY

When preparing a special meal, it is very helpful to have a mis-en-place list. All chefs have found themselves at some point in the middle of plating up a dish calling to a commis chef for the concasse and hearing the reply in shocked tones, 'What concasse?'. Service stops, the commis gets a look that could kill, or worse, and the dish suffers. Having worked up through the ranks to my present position, I can recommend a good mis-en-place list as a Bible for each menu.

Serves 4

- 6 oz spinach leaves, washed and de-stalked
- 8 lemon sole fillets (each 3 oz)
- 4 oz smoked salmon, thinly sliced
- 12 whole langoustines

for the butter sauce:

- ¼ pt fish stock
- ¼ pt white wine
- 4 oz butter
- 4 fl oz double cream

for the sauce americaine:

- 1 tsp butter
- shells from the cooked and peeled langoustines
- some parsley stalks
- 2 shallots, finely chopped
- 1 tsp tomato purée
- the heads from the 8 largest langoustines
- 1 tbsp brandy
- ¼ pt double cream

to garnish:

- 4 crescents baked puff pastry
- 1 courgette
- 4 oz fresh tomato

Poach whole the four smallest langoustines (for the garnish) for 10 minutes, taking care not to let any of the claws fall off. Remove and keep warm.

Break the heads off the remaining 8 langoustines and keep them for the sauce americaine. Blanch the tails in boiling water for 30 seconds, allow to cool slightly and peel off the shell, keeping the tail whole. Put the shells on one side for later. Make a cut right through along the middle of the tail with a pointed knife, but stop short about a centimetre from either end. Pat them gently to flatten them out, then steam for about 30 seconds, during which the tails will curl like a butterfly. Keep warm.

Blanch the spinach leaves in boiling water for 30 seconds, remove, and dry on kitchen paper. Lay out the sole fillets and spread the blanched spinach on top. Lay the smoked salmon on top of the spinach (do not season, as there will be enough salt in the smoked salmon). Sprinkle with a little white wine. Roll up each of the fillets fairly tightly, then wrap in cling film. Shortly before serving, steam the fillets (still wrapped in cling film) for 8 minutes. Keep warm.

Make the butter sauce by bringing the fish stock to the boil; add the wine and reduce a little, add the butter, and when it has melted whisk in the double cream. Keep warm.

To prepare the sauce americaine, melt the butter in the pan, add the parsley stalks, chopped shallots, tomato purée, shells and heads and cook for a few minutes over a low heat, stirring regularly. Pass the sauce through a very fine sieve to separate out the shells. Adjust the seasoning and keep warm.

Prepare the garnish by pre-cooking some small crescents of puff pastry. Peel, de-seed and finely chop the tomato. Cut thick slivers from the outside of the courgette and chop finely.

To serve, unwrap the sole spirals and cut into slices. Pour some of the butter sauce on each warm plate and sit the sole spiral in the sauce. Place two butterflied tails on the plate and coat with the sauce americaine. Decorate the butterflied tails with the diced courgette and tomato, and place small sprigs of dill or chervil around the plate.

Isle of Eriska Hotel

Paupiette of Sole with a Tomato Sauce

created by
ALAN CLARK

Serves 6

8 fillets of sole	¼ pt crème fraîche
seasoning	½ glass white wine
1 cup puréed spinach	3 egg whites

for the sauce:

1 onion	seasoning
6 tomatoes	½ glass white wine

Place 2 of the sole fillets into the magimix with salt and pepper, and mix for 2 minutes. Add the crème fraîche and spinach and mix for a further 2 minutes, then add the egg whites and mix for a final 2 minutes. Place into a dish, cover, and chill for at least an hour.

In the meantime make the sauce; chop the onion and tomato and place in a pan with the white wine. Cover and cook slowly for 10 minutes then pass through a fine sieve, season to taste, and keep hot until the fish is ready.

Remove the mousse mixture from the fridge when it is chilled. Place the 6 remaining sole fillets on a board and spread with the mousse mixture, then roll up the fillets tightly and secure. Add the wine to a large flat pan of water and bring to near boiling, then poach the fish gently for 3–5 minutes.

To serve, place the sole fillets on warm serving plates and cover with the sauce. Garnish with a sprig of mint.

Parkland Hotel and Restaurant

Roulade of Sole and Fresh Langoustine lined with Scottish Smoked Salmon with a light Lemon Butter Sauce

created by
CRAIG WILSON

This dish was first prepared for a party of Japanese tourists, known for their love of seafood. It consists of fresh shellfish married with smoked fish—a perfect combination. I have since used the recipe on countless occasions, and it has always met with great success. It is ideal too because of its versatility; with the chopping and changing of different seafoods, the end result is always the same—delicious!

Serves 4

for the mousse:

- 2 lb lemon sole fillets, skinned
- 5 egg whites
- ¼ pt single cream

for the roulade:

- 4 oz smoked salmon, sliced
- ¾ lb fresh langoustine tails, peeled
- 1 tbsp fresh chopped dill
- ½ tsp grated nutmeg

for the sauce:

- ¼ pt fish stock
- 2 fl oz white wine
- zest of 1 lemon
- ¼ pt single cream
- ½ lb butter

to garnish:

- 1 tomato, diced
- 4 sprigs fresh dill

Preheat the oven to Gas 4/350°F/180°C.

First prepare the sole mousse. Blend the sole fillets in a food processor and slowly add the egg whites with the blades still turning. Pass through a fine sieve, then mix in the single cream and chill. A useful tip is to place the blended fish in a bowl over iced water while adding the cream.

To make the roulade, lay out two sheets of cling film side by side and slightly overlapping. Spread the smoked salmon slices out over the film, making sure there are no gaps between slices. Remove the mousse from the refrigerator and add seasoning and chopped dill. Sprinkle the smoked salmon lightly with nutmeg, then spread the sole mousse evenly over the smoked salmon (use a palette knife dipped in cold water to allow you to spread the mousse quickly and evenly).

Place a line of peeled langoustines down the near side of the mousse, then from the near side slowly roll over and tuck in the edge and continue until you have a roulade shape and slowly tighten the ends of the cling film and tie in a knot. Roll in tin foil and tighten ends. Place on a deep tray quarter-filled with water, and then cook in the oven for 30–45 minutes. To check if it is cooked, place a skewer in the centre of the roulade. If it comes out hot, the roulade is ready.

Meanwhile, prepare the sauce. Reduce the fish stock by half, then add the white wine and lemon zest and reduce by a further quarter. Add the cream, and allow the mixture to come to the boil before reducing the heat to very low and allowing it to simmer. Cube the butter and slowly whisk into the sauce. When slightly thickened, strain and season.

To remove the cling film from the cooked roulade simply slice it in half; the cling film should come away easily. To serve, garnish the roulade with fresh tomato and dill and serve with a little sauce on the plate.

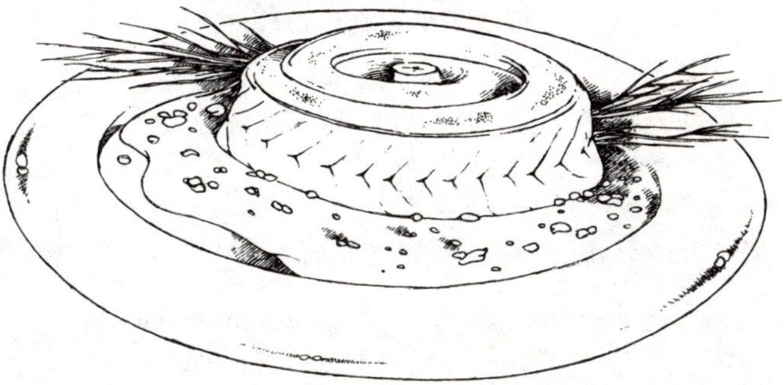

Roulade of Sole and Fresh Langoustine lined with Scottish Smoked Salmon with a light Lemon Butter Sauce

Moat House International, Glasgow

Nage of Langoustines and Scallops flavoured with Cardamom and Asparagus Tips garnished with an Inkfish Risotto

created by
THOMAS R BROWN

Serves 4

for the risotto:

- 4 oz shallots, finely diced
- 4 oz long grain rice
- 1 pt fish stock
- 2 sachets squid ink

for the nage:

- 12 langoustines, cleaned and shelled
- 12 scallops, removed from shell
- 1 pt fish stock
- 8 pieces filo pastry, cut into 4″ squares
- 12 asparagus tips, cooked
- 8 green cardamom pods, seeded
- 4 fl oz whipping cream
- 4 oz unsalted butter
- chervil sprigs

First make the risotto. Melt some butter in a pan and gently cook off the diced shallots, add the rice, and stir for a minute or two. Add the fish stock and the squid ink and cover. Cook gently until the rice is ready, then season and reserve.

To make the filo pastry parcels, butter the pastry squares and fold them in pairs over 4 dariole moulds. Cook in a hot oven until crisp then remove and reserve.

For the nage, gently cook the langoustines and scallops in the fish stock, remove and keep warm. Add the cardamom seeds to the stock and reduce, then pass the stock through a sieve, add the cream, and reheat. Add the butter when boiled.

To assemble the dish, arrange the scallops and langoustines on warm soup plates and place a filo basket filled with risotto in the centre. Heat the asparagus and arrange around the basket, then spoon over the fish stock and garnish with chervil. Serve warm with granary bread and butter.

Pan-Fried West Coast Scallops with Roquette Salad, Vegetable Relish and Beurre Blanc

created by

IAN BENNETT

The simple salad with the peppery taste of the roquette and the tartness of the vegetable relish marry wonderfully with the sweetness of the scallops, to make a superb starter or main course. It is well worth cultivating an obliging fishmonger who will prepare your scallops for you.

Chef's hint: Only use fresh scallops for this dish. Frozen scallops are usually glazed and have absorbed a lot of water, so when you come to pan-fry them, instead of being crisp and succulent, they will braise in the water that is given off and become tough and inedible.

Serves 6

6 large fresh king scallops, cleaned
½ lb roquette, washed

for the beurre blanc:

3 shallots, finely chopped
1 tbsp white wine vinegar
½ pt dry white wine
4–6 white peppercorns, cracked
8 oz unsalted butter
juice of ½ lemon
pinch cayenne pepper
sea salt

for the vinaigrette:

185ml (6½ fl oz) extra virgin olive oil
½ tsp smooth Dijon mustard
2 tbsp sherry vinegar
125ml (4½ fl oz) light vegetable oil
sea salt and pepper, to taste

for the vegetable relish:

½ red pepper
1 medium carrot
1 tbsp gherkins
1 tbsp capers
2 shallots
4 green olives, stoned
4 tbsp red wine vinegar
sea salt

First make the beurre blanc. Put the shallots, vinegar, peppercorns and wine in a pan and reduce until only about 4 tbsp of liquid remain. Strain this reduction through a fine sieve into a stainless steel or enamel pan, heat until just hot and then whisk in the butter slowly. *Do not overheat or else the sauce will split.* Now add the lemon juice, salt and cayenne pepper. The beurre blanc will keep for up to an hour, covered in a warm place.

To make the vinaigrette, put the vinegar in a small bowl with the salt and whisk until the grains have dissolved, then add the mustard and slowly and gradually whisk in the two oils. Check the seasoning and adjust as required.

For the vegetable relish, chop up all the ingredients very finely, then place in a small bowl with the vinegar, season and mix.

To assemble the salad, put the roquette leaves in a large bowl and dress with the vinaigrette. Divide the salad evenly between 6 large, tepid plates, arranging it in a nice big pile in the middle of each plate. Then put 6 small mounds of vegetable relish on each plate, evenly spaced around the edge. Slice the scallops into six slices, brush with vegetable oil on both sides, and then season. Heat a pan over a high heat and then put in the scallop slices, cooking for just 30–40 seconds on one side and 10–15 on the other. Put the scallop slices in between the vegetable relish on each plate, to give a 'clock face' effect, then dribble the warmed beurre blanc over the scallops and serve immediately.

Wine suggestion: 1992 Chablis 1er Cru 'Fourchaume', La Mansardiere. 'Fourchaume' is unmistakably the most famous of all Chablis 1er Cru. Powerful aromas, fresh and long-flavoured.

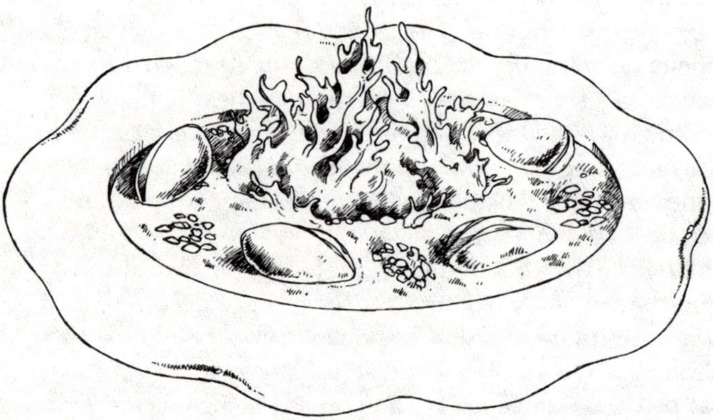

Pan-Fried West Coast Scallops with Roquette Salad, Vegetable Relish and Beurre Blanc

Three Chimneys Restaurant

Crab Tart with Lemon Butter Sauce

created by
SHIRLEY SPEAR

When we moved to this remote and beautiful corner of Skye we had no previous experience or training in running a restaurant. Our opening night in April 1985 was a nightmare. Hot Crab Tart was a starter on our first dinner menu, due to come out of the oven to coincide with opening time, but during the frantic build-up I almost let it burn. This was almost the last straw, and with no room in the chaotic kitchen I put the tart on the garden table outside the back door and declared it 'off' the menu. Eventually, however, due to the clamours of our guests, I was persuaded to bring the tart back in, reheat it and serve it. Unbelievably, it was a huge hit, and remained on our menu for several years until I got thoroughly bored with baking at least two every day! By popular request, Hot Crab Tart has recently made a comeback. The tangy Lemon Butter Sauce is a new and welcome addition, offsetting the richness of the crab.

8 oz shortcrust pastry

for the filling:

¾–1 lb mixed brown and white crabmeat
juice of ½ lemon
1 tsp Dijon mustard
salt, ground white pepper and freshly grated nutmeg
3 eggs
¼ pt double cream

for the lemon butter sauce:

6 oz unsalted butter
finely grated rind and juice of ½ lemon
2 tbsp white wine
3 egg yolks

Preheat the oven to Gas 5/375°F/190°C.

Line a 9″ flan tin with the pastry and bake blind. Meanwhile prepare the filling by mixing the crabmeat with all the seasonings. Whisk the eggs and cream together then fold the crabmeat into the egg mixture. Pour into the pre-baked flan case and return the flan to the middle shelf of the oven for 25–30 minutes until golden and just firm to touch.

For the sauce, melt the butter over a low heat. Blend the lemon, wine and egg yolks together in a liquidizer then remove the cap from the centre of the lid and pour in the butter in a steady stream through the top. Continue blending for a few seconds. reheat gently in a saucepan, without boiling, before serving. If it is too thick, or too acidic, add a little cream. Season to taste.

Serve the crab tart hot or cold with fresh salad, freshly baked wholemeal bread and a spoonful of the warm lemon butter sauce.

Ostlers Close Restaurant

Fillets of Monkfish in a Light Cheese Herb Batter on a Pesto-flavoured Sauce

created by

JAMES GRAHAM

This recipe was devised when we were looking for ideas for an Italian evening we were holding in the restaurant. Previously we had not ventured into Mediterranean-style cooking and this particular theme night opened up new avenues for us. That was several years ago, and we now use a lot more Mediterranean-style ingredients and recipes.

Chef's hints: If you have excess basil, you can make large quantities of pesto sauce, as it stores well in airtight jars in the refrigerator. Don't throw out the stalks of the basil either, as they can be used to flavour olive oil.

Serves 4

1 lb monkfish fillet
olive oil for frying

for the sauce:

3 shallots, finely chopped
4 tomatoes, skinned, deseeded and chopped
2 tbsp pesto paste (see below)
¼ pt fish stock
¼ pt white wine

for the batter:

1 oz fresh parmesan, finely grated
1 oz pecorino, grated
1 oz Jarlesberg, grated
2 eggs
2 oz flour
2 oz mixed herbs, chopped (basil, dill, chervil, chives and parsley)
seasoning
milk (to reach batter consistency)

for the pesto paste:

3 oz fresh basil leaves
¼ pt olive oil
3 tbsp pine nuts
2 cloves garlic
3 oz parmesan, grated

Place all ingredients for the pesto sauce together in a blender and process to a paste. To make the sauce, sweat off the shallots in a little olive oil, then add the tomato, 2 tbsp pesto sauce, the fish stock and the white wine. Bring to the boil, simmer for 5 minutes and season to taste. Keep the sauce warm while you prepare the batter by mixing all the ingredients together.

Cut the monkfish into slices, season, and dip each slice first in flour and then in the batter. Cook the fish in hot olive oil in a large frying pan; if the pan isn't big enough to take all the slices at once, cook them in batches and keep warm in the oven.

To serve, coat hot plates with the sauce and top with the monkfish pieces.

Fried Bairdie-Loach wi' Ridrits an' Creesh Dorty (Pan-fried Sea Bass with Fennel and Crisp Beetroot)

created by
ALAN HILL

Serves 4

for the fish stock (makes 1 litre):

1kg Dover sole bones
30g butter
60g onions, chopped
30g celery, chopped
30g fennel, chopped
30g leeks, chopped
½ bay leaf
15g dill
15g chervil
cayenne pepper
6 white peppercorns
salt and freshly ground pepper
15cl white wine
1.2ltr cold water

4 fillets of sea bass, each 160g
120g julienne of beetroot
30g shallots
15cl white wine
5cl Pernod
30cl fish stock (see above)
12 saffron threads
15g chickpeas, blanched
15g lentils, blanched
picked chervil
15g broad beans
15g chives, chopped
15g tomatoes, diced
30g paysanne of vegetables, blanched
100g julienne of fennel
100g butter
salt and freshly ground pepper
12 button onions

To make the fish stock, cut and wash the fish bones under cold running water. Remove and dry, ensuring that all the blood has been removed from the bones. Place the butter into a saucepan and cook the fish bones and vegetables without colouring. Add the herbs and peppercorns and deglaze with the white wine. Season with salt and pepper and pour in the cold water. Bring to the boil and skim, then allow the stock to cook for 20 minutes. Check the seasoning, then pass through a fine sieve and allow to cool. Use as and when required.

Season and pan-fry the sea bass in a touch of clarified butter, being careful not to overcook. Remove, dry and keep warm. Deep-fry the julienne of beetroot until crisp, then dry and keep warm. Place the shallots into a saucepan with some butter and cook without colouring. Deglaze with the white wine and Pernod, and reduce by one half, then gradually add the fish stock. Infuse the saffron threads and add the pulses, beans, chives, tomatoes and prepared vegetables. Sauté the julienne of fennel in a touch of butter and keep warm. Slowly add the butter to the stock to create a creamy velvet-looking sauce. Check the seasoning and correct if necessary. Place the sauce upon the serving plate, arranging the button onions around the dish. In the middle of each plate lay the fennel, and place the fish on top. Garnish with the chervil and crisp beetroot and serve hot and immediately.

Turnberry Hotel, Golf Courses and Spa

Fillets of Rainbow Trout and Scampi with a Sauterne, Tomato and Chervil Cream Sauce

created by
D STEWART CAMERON

Chef's hints: Use a pair of tweezers to remove fine pin bones from the fillets of trout; it will make them much more pleasant to eat.

Roll the fillets and the scampi tails as tightly as possible before cooking, as this will improve their presentation when served.

Be sure to poach the delicate trout fillets as gently as possible, to prevent them breaking up.

A little butter added to the sauce before coating the turbans will increase the richness of the dish.

Serves 4

- 8 fillets of rainbow trout, trimmed, each 3½ oz (85g)
- 8 scampi tails, picked, each 1 oz (25g)

for the sauce:

- 1 oz (25g) butter
- ¾ oz (20g) shallots, finely chopped
- 8 fl oz (250ml) dry white wine
- 1 pt (500ml) fish stock
- 13 oz (320g) tomatoes, blanched and diced
- ½ oz (15g) chives, chopped
- ¼ oz (5g) picked chervil
- 1 pt (500ml) double cream
- 1 oz (25g) hard knob of butter for working into sauce, optional

to garnish:

- 4 puff pastry crescents
- 4 cooked scampi heads

Prepare the trout fillets by removing all the bones and skin, and place the fillets flat on a clean board with the inside facing up. Lay one scampi tail over each fillet with the thick base of the scampi matching the thick edge of the fillet, then carefully roll the fillet up as tightly as possible to form a 'turban', which will then stand on its base with the small end of the scampi showing out of the top. Use two cocktail sticks inserted through the sides to hold each turban together.

Lightly butter a small sauteuse or sauté pan and sweat off the shallots, then add the white wine, reduce by half, and remove from the heat. Place the turbans in the pan, add sufficient fish stock to cover, and then place a buttered square of greaseproof paper over the top of the pan (or a tight-fitting lid) before bringing to a gentle simmer to cook the fish until tender. Remove the fillets and keep in a covered dish.

Return the pan to a high heat and reduce the sauce to really concentrate its flavour, then add half the blanched diced tomato, chives and chervil. Cook for one minute then add the double cream and reduce over a gentle heat until the mixture has the consistency of a sauce. Now pass it through a fine muslin strainer into a clean pan.

Ensure the trout turbans are hot by gently plunging them into hot fish stock for 1 minute. Meanwhile add the remainder of the chervil, chives and tomatoes to the sauce. Place the turbans carefully onto a warm plate and nappe (coat) them with the sauce. Garnish with the warm puff pastry crescents, cooked scampi heads and freshly picked chervil.

Creel Restaurant and Rooms

Fish Cakes with Lemon Butter Sauce

created by
ALAN CRAIGIE

Serves 4–6

for the lemon butter sauce:

- 8 oz butter
- juice of 1 lemon
- 2 fl oz chicken stock
- seasoning

for the fishcakes:

- 1 oz onions
- 1 oz leeks
- 1 oz butter
- ¼ pt white wine
- 8 oz salmon (tail)
- 4 oz haddock
- 4 oz hake (or any white fish)
- 12 oz mashed potato
- seasoning
- flour, egg and breadcrumbs

First make the lemon butter sauce. Chop the butter into ¼″ cubes and place in a pan with the lemon juice and chicken stock. Bring to a simmer, whisking all the time, then season. For a creamier texture blitz through a food processor at high speed for a few minutes.

To make the fishcakes, sweat the onion and leeks in the butter, add the wine and reduce to a syrup-like consistency. Cut the fish into small cubes and add to the cooked onion and leeks. Fold in 8 oz mashed potato then add the rest a spoonful at a time until you have a blended texture, and season. Make this mixture into 12–18 balls, and dip each first into flour, then eggwash and finally breadcrumbs to prepare for deep frying. Heat a pan of oil to 180°C/350°F and fry the cakes for 4–5 minutes until golden brown.

To serve, pour the warm lemon butter sauce on to individual serving dishes and place three fish cakes in the middle. Garnish with fresh herbs, for example chervil, parsley, dill etc.

Egg Tagliatelli with Wild Mushroom Sauce

created by
THE CONTINI FAMILY

Valvona & Crolla, an Aladdin's cave of a shop with wines, cheeses, olive oil, dried sausages and wild mushrooms piled from floor to ceiling, is an Edinburgh institution, and also attracts customers throughout the country. Now over 60 years old, it is still managed by the descendants of Alfonso Crolla and boasts a range of Italian produce and wine second to none in the UK. This sauce, or 'sugo', is an old favourite of the family, and it is especially tasty in the folds of the Boccolotti pasta.

Serves 4

- 1 oz (25g) dried wild porcini
- 1 small clove garlic, finely chopped
- 2 oz (50g) smoked pancetta (or smoked bacon)
- 2 tbsp shallots, finely chopped
- 2 tbsp olive oil or extra virgin olive oil
- 10 oz (300g) tin good-quality tomatoes (try San Marzano)

Soak the mushrooms in a cup of warm water for 20 minutes. Drain and reserve the liquid, then rinse the mushrooms, checking for grit. Meanwhile, sauté the shallots and garlic in the olive oil until the shallots are transparent, then add the pancetta and gently brown. Now add the strained soaking liquid, raise the heat and reduce. Finally, add the funghi and tomatoes, and simmer for 20 minutes to form a delicious thick sauce. Season as desired and serve with dry egg tagliatelli.

Strips of Chicken Homardine

created by
WILLIE MCCUTCHEON

This dish has recently been added to the evening bistro menu at the Isles of Glencoe Hotel. Its light texture and combination of flavours have been very popular with our guests.

Serves 2

- 1 chicken breast (6 oz)
- 1 oz butter
- 1 shallot, finely chopped
- ½ glass dry white wine
- 4–5 collops of freshly-cooked lobster
- ¼ pt double cream
- 2 sprigs fresh tarragon
- 1 oz lobster butter
- 4 lemon segments

Cut the chicken breast into thin strips, and cook in a sauté pan with the butter and shallot for 4–5 minutes. Add the wine and cook until reduced by half. Add to the pan the double cream, one sprig of tarragon and the collops of lobster. Cook out until the sauce begins to thicken—about 3–4 minutes. At this stage remove the chicken and lobster from the pan and keep warm.

Off the heat, gently fold the lobster butter through the cream sauce. Do not allow the sauce to re-boil after this stage, as it will split. To serve, place the chicken and lobster on a plate, coat with the sauce, and garnish with lemon segments and fresh tarragon.

Andrea's Camp-fire Chicken

created by
ANN NICOLL

My daughters, Nicola and Andrea, both passed the rigorous selection procedure for Raleigh; Andrea went on expedition to Panama, and Nicola to Australia. Nicola is a great cook, but Andrea never cooks unless she has to. However, this is her favourite way to cook chicken, which must mean that anyone can cope with it! The mustard and oatmeal protect the tender texture of the chicken, guaranteeing even the most inexperienced cook success. It can be cooked over a camp-fire, but I often prepare it for our restaurant, and it is always enjoyed.

1 breast of chicken per person
French mustard (or mild grain mustard)
medium oatmeal (NOT porridge oats!)
butter

Spread the chicken breasts generously with the mustard, then coat with oatmeal. Make sure the meat is well covered. Heat a knob of butter in a frying pan and fry the breasts for about 10 minutes, turning them several times. Check with a sharp knife at the thickest part to see if the meat is thoroughly cooked, before serving on a hollandaise sauce with vegetables, or on a tossed salad with vinaigrette.

Wood Pigeon with Honey and Chestnut Sauce

created by
NEIL ROSS

Serves 4

4 wood pigeons
1 pt water
2 oz shallots, finely chopped
4 oz chestnuts, finely chopped
3 × ¼ gill measures whisky
2 tsp honey
vegetable oil
2 oz butter

Remove the breasts from the pigeons and set aside. Place the carcasses in the oven for 10 minutes at Gas 3/325°F/160°C to roast until brown. When nicely roasted, put in a pot and cover with cold water, then bring to the boil and reduce by half. This will be used as the stock for the chestnut and honey sauce.

Sauté the shallots and chestnuts in a little butter for a few minutes, add the whisky and flame. Add the pigeon stock and reduce by half again. Finally, add the honey and seasoning to finish the sauce.

Season the wood pigeon breasts and sauté in a little oil and butter for about 10 minutes. Once cooked, slice the meat onto dinner plates, coat with the sauce, and serve.

Roast Breast of Wood Pigeon with Girolles and Foie Gras

created by
DAVID R BATES

Serves 4

4 wood pigeons
4 slices streaky bacon
350g large potatoes
salt and pepper
40g clarified butter
2 tbsp oil
25g unsalted butter
16 girolles (chanterelles)
2 artichoke bottoms, cooked and cut into 16 wedges
120ml Madeira
350ml brown chicken stock
4 slices foie gras
sprigs of thyme to garnish

Preheat the oven to Gas 8/450°F/230°C.

Remove the legs and wishbones from the pigeons. Place a slice of bacon over the breasts of each pigeon and tie into place. Peel the potatoes, then cut into fine strips using a mandolin or by hand. Season the potato and mix with the clarified butter. Divide the potato into four and form into cake shapes; fry these gently until golden brown on both sides, then keep them warm.

Lightly season the inside cavity of the pigeons. Heat the oil, then add half the butter and sear the pigeons in the hot fat. Place them on one breast in a tray and roast them for 3 minutes, turn onto the other breast and roast for a further 3 minutes, and finally turn the birds on their backs for another 3 minutes. Remove and keep warm.

Carefully wipe the girolles clean to remove any dirt. Pour off the fat from the pan and add the remaining butter. Fry the girolles and artichoke wedges over a gentle heat, then remove from the pan. Pour off the fat and add the Madeira, reduce by half, then add the stock and reduce by half again, and finally strain through muslin.

To serve, remove the breasts from the pigeons and keep warm along with the girolles, artichokes and potato cakes. Heat a dry frying pan, season the foie gras, and quickly fry for 10 seconds on each side. Place a potato cake in the centre of each plate and top each one with a slice of foie gras. Place two pigeon breasts on top of these and arrange the girolles and artichokes around the plate, alternating them. Spoon a little sauce over the breasts and pour the rest onto the plates. Finish the dish off with a few sprigs of thyme.

Pigeon, Roast Roots and Juniper

created by
ANDREW RADFORD

Potato stacks are an impressive accompaniment to this dish; place slices of raw potato on top of each other to form stacks approximately 1½" high, brush with olive oil and season, and bake for up to 30 minutes with the vegetables.

Wine suggestion: Chateauneuf-du-Pape, Clos des Papes (1991), Paul Avril

Serves 4

4 pigeons
olive oil
8 oz carrot
6 oz parsnip
6 oz celeriac
6 oz swede
10 shallots
6 oz leek
1 pt stock (from pigeon carcasses)
1 tsp juniper berries
salt and pepper
2 oz parsley

Remove the breasts from the pigeons and place them in oil (this can be done up to 10 days before cooking). Make up the stock using the carcasses.

Dice the carrot, parsnip, celeriac, swede, shallots and leek, and sweat off together in olive oil in a thick-bottomed pan. Then place the root vegetables in a high oven for 15–20 minutes to roast until cooked.

Meanwhile, reduce the stock with the juniper berries in a clean pan until a light infusion results, then season. Pan-fry the pigeon breasts for 1 minute on both sides. Put a lid on the pan and put to one side.

On each of 4 serving plates place a potato stack and some roast roots. Position the pigeon breasts on the roots. Add a little sauce and sprinkle with finely chopped parsley. Serve.

Balgonie House

Warm Galantine of Grouse with Braised Lentils

created by
DAVID HINDMARCH

This recipe was designed to show the versatility of the finest of game birds, the young grouse. Sadly, spring frosts and over-zealous shooting have depleted their numbers in recent years. If you are unable to obtain young grouse, therefore, this recipe will work just as well with wood pigeon. In this case, you should reduce the cooking time to 12 minutes.

Serves 4

for the galantine of grouse:

- 5 young grouse
- 1 large carrot
- 1 medium onion
- 1 stick celery
- 1 small leek (white section only)
- 2 pints chicken stock
- 1 tbsp redcurrant jelly
- ¼ pt Madeira
- 1 egg white
- ¼ pt double cream
- 1 tsp chopped chives

for the braised lentils:

- 8 rashers back bacon
- 1 tsp chopped marjoram
- 1 tsp chopped sage
- 2 oz brown lentils
- 1 pt chicken stock
- 1 large carrot, split in half
- 1 onion, quartered
- 1 stick celery
- small sprig thyme

To prepare the grouse, remove the breasts from the bird and set on one side then roughly chop the carcasses. Roughly chop the carrot, onion, celery and leek, heat a little oil in a casserole and brown the carcasses and vegetables together. Place the carcasses and vegetables together in a large saucepan with the chicken stock, bring to the boil, and skim the surface to remove any scum. Simmer slowly, covered, for 1½ hours, then strain into a clean saucepan. Over a high heat, reduce the sauce to half a pint, then add the redcurrant jelly and Madeira and once again reduce to half a pint. Season to taste.

Meanwhile, place 2 grouse breasts in a food processor goblet together with the egg white and a little salt and pepper. Blend to a purée and place in a chilled bowl, then stir in the double cream and chopped herbs.

To assemble the galantines, take 2 rashers of bacon and stretch them as thinly as possible with the back of a knife. Lay the rashers on a board, overlapping slightly, then place 2 grouse breasts in the centre. Spread a quarter of the mousse down the centre of the breasts, then bring over the ends of the bacon to form a tidy parcel. Carefully transfer the galantine onto an 8″ square of buttered tin foil and wrap tightly to resemble a Christmas cracker. Repeat with the remaining breasts to form 4 galantines altogether. Chill the parcels for 30 minutes. At this stage, preheat the oven to Gas 8/450°F/230°C.

In the meantime, pick over the lentils carefully and wash them. Place in a pan together with the chicken stock, vegetables, thyme and a little salt. Bring to the boil then simmer for approximately 15 minutes, until just cooked.

To cook the galantines, fill a roasting tray with boiling water to the depth of 1″. Place the galantines into the tray and bake for 15 minutes, turning the parcels after 8 minutes. Remove the parcels from the water and allow them to rest in a warm place for 10 minutes.

To serve, remove the vegetables from the lentils and discard. Using a slotted spoon, drain the lentils and scatter them over the warm serving plates. Unwrap the galantines and carve them into half-inch slices, and arrange in a semi-circle over the lentils. Finally, surround with a generous amount of Madeira wine and serve.

Finally, give yourself a pat on the back and pour yourself a dram—you've earned it!

Auchterarder House

Gamefowl and Deer

created by
DAVID JAMES HUNT MCGB

This recipe was created for the Salon Culinière Glasgow 1993, a meat and whisky event broadcast live, where it won the Haig trophy and gold medal. It is a combination of red deer and young guinea fowl with a whisky, pickled walnut and thyme sauce.

Serves 4

- 2 oz smoked bacon
- 2 oz brown lentils
- 1 oz cooking barley
- mirepoix of carrot, celery and onion
- bones from saddle
- 2 young guinea fowl
- 6–8 oz red deer loin
- large measure malt whisky
- dash Crabbies Ginger Wine
- 10 fl oz jellied game stock
- 2 juniper berries
- ½ bunch fresh thyme
- 8 baby parsnips
- 8 finger carrots
- 8 small shallots
- 2 oz cold unsalted butter
- pinch sugar
- 2 pickled walnuts

First dice the bacon and cook it with the lentils in half the game stock until tender, then add the barley and keep warm. Meanwhile prepare the parsnips, carrots and shallots for glazing. Remove the wishbone from the fowl, brown the mirepoix and bones in hot oil, and then seal the guinea fowl and venison quickly. Season the meat, cook until just underdone, then remove and keep warm. Remove the excess fat from the pan, and deglaze with whisky, ginger wine, game stock, walnut shells, junipers and half the thyme, then reduce. Place the prepared parsnips, carrots and shallots in boiling water with the butter and sugar and cook until glazed, then remove and keep warm.

Place ring moulds onto warm plates and spoon the pulse mixture into them. For the guinea fowl, remove the bone and skin from the thigh and place it on top of the pulse mix and remove the breasts and place them down one side of the pulses. Carve the venison loin and place it down the opposite side (use the trimmings for the sauce).

Season and taste the sauce, then strain through muslin. Reheat the vegetables and scatter round the dish (flash if required to reheat), then nappe with the sauce and finish with the diced pickled walnuts and the remaining fresh thyme.

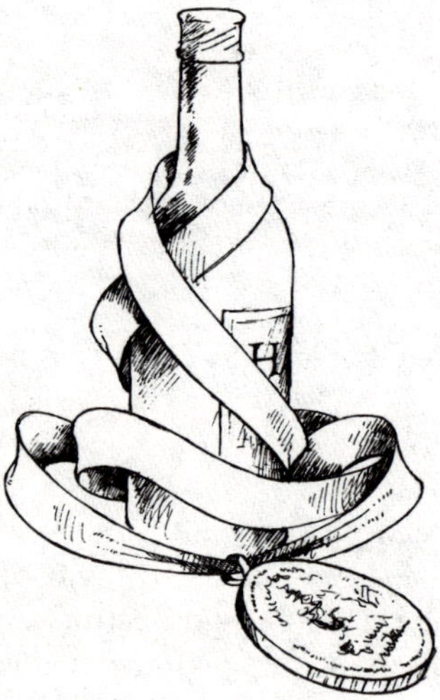

Glasgow Hilton Hotel

Medley of Highland Game with Forest Mushrooms on a Rich Game Jus

created by
MICHAEL MIZZEN

'Camerons' at the Glasgow Hilton has been recreated in the style of the Clan Cameron hunting-lodge, complete with stalking gear and Gun Room. The kitchen reflects the high quality of the Scottish produce available, cooked in a thoroughly modern fashion, and this dish is a classic example of Camerons' style. All areas of Scotland produce their own typical 'stovied' recipes, and at Camerons we enjoy the game from the hills and valleys of Lochaber.

In this recipe, the cooking style has been modernized to retain the richness of the mature game, and the potato and stock elements lightened to contrast with the meats. All in all, this is a dish the Clanschief would have been delighted to serve to his kinsfolk after a hard day's hunting.

Serves 2

for the medley of game:

- 1 quail
- 1 pigeon
- 8 oz venison fillet
- 2 oz chicken farce

for the sauce:

- 10 fl oz port wine
- 10 fl oz chicken stock
- sprig of rosemary
- sprig of thyme
- bay leaf
- mirepoix (1 oz shallots, 1 oz carrots, 1 oz celery, 2 cloves garlic, 1 oz leek, all diced)

to garnish:

- 2 oz mixed wild mushrooms
- 1 oz potato
- 1 oz tomatoes
- 1 oz mixed flat parsley and chervil

Preheat oven to Gas 5/375°F/190°C.

Remove all the meats from the bone, then place bones and mirepoix together in a dish in the oven for 20 minutes. In the meantime, joint the quail and trim all the meats, stuff the pigeon with chicken farce as required, and place in the refrigerator to chill. Dice the potato and tomato into approximately 1cm cubes, lightly wash the mushrooms, and place all these vegetables on kitchen paper to absorb the excess moisture. Place the sprigs of fresh herbs in iced water to refresh them before starting the sauce. Most of the work is now done, so have a celebratory sip of wine.

For the sauce, remove the cooked bones and mirepoix from the oven (but don't turn the oven off yet!) and place in a large pan. Over a high heat, add the port wine and chicken stock and reduce the sauce, removing the fat as it surfaces. This should take about 10 minutes. When the sauce is properly reduced, pass it through a fine strainer into a clean pan and season lightly.

In a non-stick pan, quickly fry all the meat portions to seal them and then place in the oven for 5 minutes. In the same pan, sauté the diced potato until golden brown. Now you can begin assembling the dish; place the potato, tomato and wild mushrooms together in the centre of a serving plate and remove the meat from the oven. Place the quail legs and breasts on the mushrooms, slice the venison fillet and pigeon and arrange them outside the mushrooms. Finally add the sauce around the mushrooms and meat, garnish with flat parsley and chervil, and serve immediately.

Roastit Hurdie o' Venison wi' a Briest o' Magret wi' Tatties an' Neeps (Seared Loin of Perthshire Venison served with Sliced Duckling and Gin Sauce)

created by
ALAN HILL

It is well worth planning your menu in plenty of time, to allow the venison loin to marinade for a whole day.

Serves 4

for the marinade:

60cl red wine
15cl Madeira
100g mirepoix (cooked diced vegetables)
15g ginger
1 bouquet garni
salt and freshly ground black pepper

for the game gravy (makes 1 litre):

300g pheasant trimmings (legs)
30g butter
5cl oil
60g shallots, chopped
15g carrots, chopped
30g celery, chopped
10cl white wine
5cl Calvados
½ bayleaf
5g rosemary
60g tomatoes
15g tomato purée
1.2ltr game stock
salt and freshly ground black pepper

for the turnip cakes:

250g shredded potato
250g shredded turnip
salt, pepper and nutmeg
2cl oil
60g butter
15g chopped fines herbes

- 5cl olive oil
- rosemary
- 1 trimmed and marinated loin of venison, 400g
- 2 Magret duck breasts, each 150g
- salt and freshly ground black pepper
- 10cl gin
- 15cl red wine
- 5g juniper berries
- 30cl game gravy (see above)
- 120g garden vegetables
- sugar and nutmeg
- 60g butter to finish

Mix all the ingredients for the marinade together in a bowl, and marinade the venison for 24 hours.

To make the game gravy, place the meat trimmings into some hot oil and cook until brown. Remove, dry, and discard the excess fat. Place some butter in a saucepan and cook the chopped vegetables until golden brown. Add the meat trimmings and cook for a further 5 minutes. Deglaze with the wine and Calvados, then add the herbs, tomatoes and tomato purée. Slowly add the game stock and skim thoroughly. Season. Once the correct consistency and flavour is reached, remove and pass through a sieve. Keep until required.

Next make the turnip cakes. Wash the shredded potato thoroughly under cold running water to remove all the excess starch, remove and dry. In a stainless steel bowl mix the potato and turnip together. Season with the salt, pepper, a touch of nutmeg and the herbs. Place the oil and butter into a non-stick pan and place a ring in the centre. Press a quarter of the potato mix into the ring and cook until golden brown on both sides, then repeat with the rest of the mix to give four cakes.

To cook the meat, place the oil and rosemary into a frying pan and cook the seasoned venison and duckling to taste, ensuring that the fat on the duckling is crisp. Remove, dry and keep warm. Discard the cooking fat from the pan and deglaze with the gin and red wine, reducing by one half. Add the juniper berries and then gradually add the game gravy, reducing by a further half. Reheat the turnip cakes and cook the garden vegetables, and season the vegetables with a touch of sugar and nutmeg.

Pass the sauce through a fine strainer and replace on the heat. Whisk in the butter, and check the seasoning and consistency.

To serve, slice the duckling into thin strips and the venison loin into four pieces. Pour the sauce onto hot serving dishes and lay a turnip cake on top of each, lay the duckling around the cake and place a venison piece on top. Garnish the dish with garden vegetables and serve immediately.

The Grill Room, Sheraton Grand Hotel, Edinburgh

Ayrshire Spring Lamb with Stovies

created by

JEAN-MICHEL GAUFFRE

'You can't have stovies on the menu of a five-star hotel restaurant—it's OK for the staff, but that's about it!'

I remember that chefs' meeting a few weeks before the opening of our Grill Room at the Sheraton Grand. We were trying to identify Scottish recipes and products that would impart to our new restaurant the exclusivity we were after. About a year later, Ayrshire Lamb with Stovies is still on our à la carte menu, and still one of our top sellers! At home, the same technique could be applied to beef, pork or game. For a lower budget but still sensational meal, try it with herb sausages.

Serves 4

5 lb rack of spring lamb
2 medium carrots
2 stalks celery
1 leek
1 bay leaf
1 sprig thyme, chopped
1 sprig rosemary, chopped
1 clove garlic, crushed
1½ lb potatoes
1 onion, chopped
1 tbsp plain flour
2 oz butter

First remove the loins of lamb from the bones, and ensure all the sinews and fat are removed as well. You should end up with two very lean pieces of meat. Clean all the bones, and separate the fat from the meat of the flanks.

To prepare a lamb stock, roast the lamb bones in a large dish in a moderate oven until browned. Dice the carrots, celery and leek roughly and add to the bones, along with the flour, crushed garlic and half of the herbs, and roast for a few more minutes in the oven. Remove from the oven and place in a large pan along with water to cover, and cook slowly, taking time to skim the stock. Strain when ready and reserve.

In the meantime, peel the potatoes and dice to ¼" (½cm) cubes. Melt a knob of butter in a pan and add some finely chopped lamb flank, and fry until well coloured. Add the onion and the rest of the herbs and cook for a few more minutes before adding the cubed potato. When the potato starts to colour, add enough lamb stock to cover and cook until the stock evaporates completely and the potatoes are soft. Reduce the remaining stock until it forms a sauce just thick enough to coat the back of a spoon. Strain, season and reserve.

Season the lamb fillets and seal them quickly in a pan with a knob of butter over a high heat (they should remain pink inside).

To assemble the dish, place the stovies off-centre on a warm serving plate (using a cup or small mould). Slice the lamb and arrange around the stovies, pour some sauce around and serve immediately. Buttered fresh market vegetables or a tossed side salad complement this dish very nicely.

Thainstone House Hotel and Country Club

Roast Loin of Scotch Lamb with Wild Mushroom Tarragon Mousse on a Rosti Potato with Rosemary Sauce

created by
BILL GIBB

Serves 4

2 best ends of lamb
(1½ kg, bone in)
200g potatoes
50ml olive oil
50g flageolet beans
100g baby carrots
100g button mushrooms
50g wild mushrooms
50g clarified butter
4 herb bouquets

for the wild mushroom mousse:
150g chicken breast
1 egg
pinch seasoning
150ml double cream
2 sprigs tarragon
100g wild mushrooms

for the rosemary sauce:
veal bones
50g mirepoix of
vegetables
1 clove garlic
50ml white wine
50ml Madeira wine
750ml clear chicken stock
sprig rosemary
25g butter

Bone out the best ends of lamb, remove all fat and sinews, then cut to give 4 equal portions. Seal quickly in oil, then allow to cool. Finely chop the lamb bones for the sauce.

To make the mousse, blend the chicken breasts in a food processor and pass through a fine sieve into a clean bowl over ice. Add the egg and seasoning, then gradually incorporate the double cream with the chopped tarragon and diced wild mushrooms. Pipe the mousse on top of each lamb portion, then wrap with crepinette and place in the refrigerator.

Sweat down the veal bones with the mirepoix of vegetables and garlic and then deglaze with the white wine and Madeira. Reduce, then add the chicken stock and rosemary, and simmer gently for 15–20 minutes, skimming all the time. Pass the sauce through fine muslin into a clean pan.

Prepare all the vegetables; blanch the flageolet beans, trim the carrots and wild mushrooms before cooking, and roast the button onions until golden brown.

For the potato rosti, grate the potatoes and sweat down in clarified butter and a little water for 4 minutes. Drain in a colander, then press down into four lightly greased rosti moulds and fry until crisp and golden brown.

Roast the lamb portions at Gas 5/375°F/190°C for 6 minutes. Glaze under a salamander oven (or a hot domestic grill) until the mousse is golden brown. Rest on a cooling rack before service.

Meanwhile, bring the sauce to first boil and finish with the hard butter, and reheat the vegetables for garnish.

To serve, place the rosti potato in the centre of each dish, and crown with the roast loin. Arrange the carrots, wild mushrooms, button onions and flageolet beans around each portion. Finish with the sauce and a herb bouquet.

The Gleneagles Hotel

Clapshott Lamb

created by
ALAN HILL

Serves 4

for the lamb stock (makes 1 litre):

1.5kg lamb bones
30g butter
60g onion
30g carrot
30g leeks
30g celery
60g tomato purée
15cl red wine
½ bayleaf
thyme leaves
10g rosemary
30g ginger
1.2ltr cold water
½ onion, skin on and blackened
salt and freshly ground pepper

12 lamb cutlets, each 75g
salt and pepper
5cl oil
30g butter
15g garlic purée
500g onions, sliced
500g sliced potato
15g clarified butter
nutmeg and mace
50g lamb stock (see above)
100g black pudding
chopped parsley to finish

To make the lamb stock, cut and roast the bones in the oven until golden brown. Remove from the tray and discard any excess oil or fat. Place the butter in a saucepan and cook the vegetables until golden brown. Add the tomato purée and cook for a further 5 minutes. Pour in the red wine and deglaze, cook for a further 5 minutes. Add the herbs, rosemary and ginger and pour in the cold water. Bring to the boil and skim, allow to simmer for 1 hour, place in the blackened onion. Check seasoning and then pass through a fine sieve. Use as and when required.

Season and seal the trimmed lamb cutlets in a little hot oil, remove, dry and keep warm. Discard any excess oil and add some butter to the cooking pan. Add the garlic and sliced onions and cook until golden brown. Sauté the potatoes in a touch of butter and season with salt, freshly ground pepper, and a touch of mace and nutmeg. Layer the meat, black pudding and potatoes together and nappe each layer with a touch of the lamb stock. Make the last layer of potatoes only, and brush with melted butter. Bake in a moderate oven for 1½ hours until the meat is tender and the potatoes golden brown. Serve immediately with spring-time cabbage and button onions.

Fillet of Angus Beef Resting on a Potato Rosti with a Cannelloni of Leek and Haggis

created by
PAUL WHITECROSS

This beef dish brings together the classic Scottish marriage of haggis, neeps and tatties into a modern recipe. I adapted the recipe in 1993 for a Scottish Television programme. The haggis should be cooked in advance and kept warm if possible; it will roll into a cannelloni much more easily.

Serves 4

for the leek and haggis cannelloni:

1 leek
1 haggis, cooked

for the red wine sauce:

4 shallots, chopped
2 cloves garlic, sliced
2 fl oz non-scented oil
2 fl oz red wine vinegar
5 fl oz port
½ bottle red wine
½ pt vegetable stock
½ pt good meat stock
sprigs of thyme, tarragon, parsley and a bayleaf

for the potato rosti:

4 medium-sized potatoes
salt and pepper to season
4 fillets of beef, each 6 oz
20 chantrelle mushrooms
4 tbsp non-scented oil
2 tbsp clarified butter
4 fl oz non-scented oil or 2 fl oz non-scented oil and 2 fl oz clarified butter
1 turnip

First prepare the leek cannelloni. Cut the leek into 3¾" (8cm) lengths and slit these open lengthways. Blanch in boiling water for about 3–4 minutes, remove, and cool instantly in iced water. Then drain the slices, pat them dry and retain 15 of the best large leaves. On a piece of tin foil lay 2 leaves side by side, overlapping slightly. Top them with 3 tbsp of haggis and roll them into a sausage shape, twisting the tin foil tightly at both ends to secure it. Repeat 3 more times to make 4 cannelloni in total. Set these to one side; they should be reheated later in a steamer for 6–8 minutes.

Next prepare the red wine sauce. Sweat the shallots and garlic in the non-scented oil and cook until caramelized, then deglaze by adding the red wine vinegar and reduce until completely evaporated. Add the port and red wine, bring to the boil, and reduce to about two-thirds before adding the vegetable and meat stocks. Again return to the boil, then add the herbs and simmer for 20–30 minutes, skimming continuously to remove any scum from the surface. At the end of this time pass the sauce through a sieve 3 or 4 times to make it as clear as possible, and retain it ready for use. This sauce can also be frozen for up to 2 months. It will be reduced again just before serving.

To prepare the turnip barrels, first peel the turnip then cut it as neatly as possible into 20 2″ (5cm) lengths. With a small knife, trim these pieces into barrel or olive shapes. Cook the barrels in boiling water in a sauté pan for about 25 minutes to keep them *al dente* (with a little bite).

To cook the potato rosti, wash the potatoes and then peel them (this avoids washing out the starch which will be needed to hold the rosti together). Grate on a mandoline or Japanese spaghetti machine (you can use a normal grater but this often results in the potato being mushy when cooked). Pat dry, or wrap the potato in a clean cloth to extract any water, then season with salt and pepper.

Heat the oil and clarified butter in four individual metal rosti pans or a large heavy-bottomed frying pan over a moderate heat. Add the grated potato when the oil is spitting (if using one large pan, press the potato into four individual muffin moulds, or cook one large rosti then cut it with a pastry cutter). Cook the potato until it starts to go crisp, then remove the rings and turn the rostis over to crisp the other side. Once cooked, use a piece of kitchen paper to soak up the excess oil then place the rostis on a wire rack to retain their crispness, otherwise they will start to soak up their own grease and go soft. If necessary, the rostis can be reheated in the oven for a few minutes.

At this point, return the sauce to the heat and reduce by half, then incorporate a knob of butter, check the taste and season if necessary. Pass it through a sieve into a jug ready for use.

Add the clarified butter or non-scented oil to a little sauté pan and cook the chantrelle mushrooms for about 40 seconds. Season with salt and pepper, then season the beef. Heat 2 fl oz of non-scented oil in a medium-sized sauté pan until almost smoking, then add the beef fillets and cook on both sides until medium rare.

To assemble the dish, place a potato rosti in the middle of each of 4 warm plates, and top with the beef fillet. Unwrap the cannelloni parcels, cut in half and place on top of the beef. Arrange the chantrelles and turnip around the plate, and spoon the sauce around but not over the beef. Finally place a sprig of chervil on each turnip barrel and serve.

Pavarotti Beef Stew

created by

JEFF BLAND

When Pavarotti dined at Cameron House he had polenta, salad and fresh bread with his stew—and sang very well on it!

Serves 4

- 1 lb lean stewing beef roughly cubed
- salt and pepper to season
- 4 fl oz oil
- 2 oz carrot, diced
- 2 oz onion, diced
- 2 oz celery, diced
- 2 oz leeks, diced
- 2 oz tomato purée
- 2 oz plain flour
- 1 glass red wine
- 4 pt beef stock
- 2 cloves garlic, crushed
- bayleaf
- 4 sprigs thyme
- 4 rashers bacon, cut into strips
- 4 oz mushrooms, cut into quarters

Preheat oven to low.

Warm a heavy casserole dish on the hob then add the oil and heat until it begins to smoke slightly (season the beef in the meantime). Fry the beef until brown, add the diced vegetables and brown them also, then add the tomato purée and cook for another 2–3 minutes. Mix in the flour and cook over a gentle heat for another 2–3 minutes, then slowly stir in the red wine and beef stock. Add the crushed garlic and herbs.

Cover the casserole and cook slowly for 2½–3 hours. When cooked, remove the meat and sieve the sauce. Replace the meat and check seasoning and consistency, then add the mushrooms and bacon and bring to the boil to cook them out, and SERVE!

Roast Haunch of Wild Boar

created by
MR MCCAFFREY

Two young Americans were looking at the menu and discussing what to order. One asked the other if he would share a Chateaubriand with him. The second replied, 'No, thank you. I don't drink wine.'

⅛ pt orange liqueur
2 bay leaves
2 tbsp peppercorns
2 tbsp juniper berries
4 cloves
2 cinnamon sticks

haunch of wild boar
grated peel of 1 orange
1 ltr (1¾ pt) red wine
mixed with a little water
2 tbsp vinegar

Marinade the haunch in all the other ingredients for a day, keeping it covered and turning it every so often. Remove and dry the haunch well, then season. Heat some oil in a roasting pan on top of the cooker and brown the meat all over, then sieve the marinade, add to the pan, and cover. Place in the oven at Gas 3/325°F/160°C and roast for the same time as an equivalent weight of pork. Strain the sauce and adjust the seasoning, using mixed spice, salt and pepper, and sweeten with a little sugar if desired.

Serve with spiced candied apples or glazed fruit (whatever is in season).

The Gleneagles Hotel

Musselburgh Pie

created by

ALAN HILL

This traditional Scottish pie consists of steak, oysters and mussels in oatmeal pastry.

Serves 4

for the puff pastry (makes 1kg):

40g butter
400g strong flour
8g salt
200ml water
440g butter
80g flour

for the beef stock (makes 1 litre):

1.5kg beef bones
30g butter
60g onion, chopped
30g carrot, chopped
30g leek, chopped
30g celery, chopped
60g tomato purée
15cl red wine
½ bay leaf
30g ginger
10g rosemary
salt and freshly ground pepper
1.2ltr cold water
½ onion, skin on and blackened

500g mussels, de-bearded
600g rump steak
10cl oil
30g butter
rosemary
thyme
300g onions, chopped
5g garlic, chopped
5cl red wine
15cl beef stock (see above)
15cl beef jus
16 oysters
10g parsley, chopped
400g oatmeal puff pastry (see above)
1 egg
toasted oatmeal

First make the pastry. Rub in the 40g of butter with the 400g strong flour and salt. Add the water and knead to a smooth dough. Leave to rest for 30 minutes in the refrigerator.

Meanwhile mix together the second butter and flour. Pin out the rested dough and place the butter mix over two-thirds of its surface, then fold in giving four double turns, allowing the dough to rest for an hour between each turn. Use as required, allowing the dough to rest for an hour after rolling out.

To make the beef stock, cut and roast the bones in the oven until golden brown. Remove from the tray and discard the excess fat. Melt the butter in a saucepan and brown the vegetables until golden. Add the tomato purée and cook for a further 5 minutes, then add the red wine and cook for another 5 minutes. Add the herbs, rosemary and ginger, season, and pour in the cold water. Bring back to the boil and skim, allow to simmer for an hour, place in the blackened onion. Check seasoning and then pass through a fine sieve. Use as and when required.

Steam the fresh mussels and allow to cool; take out of their shells. Trim and cut the steak into cubes, season and brown in hot oil and butter with herbs and reserve. Heat a pan and brown the onions and garlic, deglaze with red wine, then pour in the stock and reduce by half. Add the beef jus, return the steak to pan and cook until tender; allow to cool. Shell the oysters, keeping the juice. Place the meat in a suitable dish, fold the mussels into the mixture, then arrange the oysters on top and pour over the oyster juice and chopped parsley. Top with puff pastry and egg wash, then sprinkle with toasted oatmeal. Bake in a hot oven for 30–40 minutes. Serve while hot.

Desserts

Carrageen Jelly with Fresh Raspberries

created by
SUE BLOCKEY

Carrageen (sea moss or Irish moss) is found on the mid-tide line. It needs to be washed well in several changes of water. When well dried, it should be stored in a paper bag hung in a cool larder. It is rich in vitamin content, and the prepared form is obtainable from most good health food shops. Raspberries grow so well on Mull, both cultivated and wild, and it is delightful to pick your own carrageen and raspberries for a really home-produced dish!

Serves 4

1 cup carrageen, tightly packed
1 pint water
2 oz sugar
peel of 1 lemon
1 egg white
¼ pt cream, whipped to soft peaks
few drops vanilla essence

Steep the carrageen in water to cover for 10 minutes, and then drain. Simmer for 20–25 minutes in a pint of water with the sugar and lemon peel. Strain and let it cool slightly. Meanwhile whip the egg white to stiff peaks and combine with the cream, then mix well into the carrageen liquid and heat *gently* to just under boiling point. Stir in a few drops of vanilla essence and pour into a mould freshly rinsed with cold water. Allow to chill and set.

To serve, turn out the jelly and serve with fresh raspberries or fruit of your choice.

Cameron House Hotel and Country Estate

Malt Whisky Souffle Mousse

created by

JEFF BLAND

This delicious mousse will keep chilled for up to 48 hours, or frozen for 2 weeks.

- 250ml milk
- 100g sugar
- 4 egg yolks
- 400ml double cream, whipped
- 1 tsp vanilla essence
- 4 leaves gelatine (or ¼ oz gelatine powder)
- 110ml malt whisky

Boil the milk with half the sugar, and mix the rest of the sugar with the egg yolks and cream. Gradually add the boiled milk to the yolk mixture, continually beating in to mix. Return to a clean saucepan and cook over a low heat to give a custard. Add the dissolved gelatine and vanilla essence, and mix in well. Strain the custard into a bowl and cool, stirring now and again. Add the whisky.

Meanwhile, tie a double-thickness strip of greaseproof paper round the outside of individual ramekin dishes, securing with string or a rubber band. When the custard begins to thicken and set, fold in the whipped cream, a third at a time. Pour or spoon the mixture into the ramekins, filling to the top of the greaseproof paper, and chill in the refrigerator for 3–4 hours.

When set, take out of the refrigerator and carefully remove the greaseproof paper. Coat the sides of the mousse above the ramekin with toasted oatmeal, coconut or pistachio nuts.

One Devonshire Gardens

Cappuccino Brulée

created by
KEN MCCULLOCH

This fabulously rich dessert should be served in tea cups or coffee cups.

Serves 4

8 egg yolks
½ lb sugar
½ ltr (1 pt) cream
1 vanilla pod
1 tbsp coffee

Cream the egg yolks and sugar together, and bring the cream and vanilla pod to the boil. Whisk the egg yolks and sugar in a bowl over boiling water until the mixture is of a creamy consistency, then add the cream, vanilla pod and coffee to the egg mixture and whisk together. Return this mixture to the heat for 2 minutes, until it is thick enough to coat the back of a spoon, and then remove from the heat and pour into serving cups.

Set these cups in a deep dish half-filled with water, and cook in a low oven for 40 minutes until the top has hardened to the touch. Leave to cool for 4 hours. Before serving, decorate with cream whipped with icing sugar to make it extra thick and smooth.

Duo of Poached Pear in Red and White Wine

created by

NEIL ROSS

The contrasting pearly white and pink of the pear slices makes an unusual and very attractive dessert.

Serves 4

4 pears
1 pt water
1 tbsp sugar
pinch cinnamon
juice of 2 lemons
¼ bottle white wine
¼ bottle red wine
segments of 1 orange
zest of 1 orange
3 oz hazelnuts, halved

Place half the quantities of water, sugar, cinnamon and lemon juice into 2 separate pans then add the red wine to one pan and the white wine to the other.

Peel and core the pears, putting 2 into each pan, then bring to the boil and simmer for about 15 minutes. If the pears are ripe, cooking time should be reduced. Allow the pears to cool standing in the wine stock.

Remove the pears from the pans, slice and arrange attractively on plates. Garnish with orange segments, orange zest and hazelnuts. Finally, flood the plate with the red wine cooking stock and serve.

Minmore House Hotel

Raspberry and Almond Pavlova Roulade

created by

BELINDA LUXMOORE

Minmore House is distinguished by a lack of TVs, a world-famous malt whisky collection, four acres of restful gardens in the glorious Grampian region around Glenlivet, and of course its inspired and indulgent food. This roulade should be made and enjoyed on the same day.

Serves 8–10

- 8 egg whites, at room temperature
- 8 oz caster sugar
- 1 tsp white vinegar
- 1 tsp vanilla essence
- 3 oz nibbed almonds
- 1 pt double cream
- 1 lb Scottish raspberries

Preheat oven to Gas 2–3/300°F/150°C.

Whisk the egg whites until good and stiff then fold in the caster sugar and the white vinegar and vanilla essence. Carefully line a 12″ × 15″ Swiss roll tin with bakewell paper (or another non-stick baking parchment), smooth the mixture into it and sprinkle with the nibbed almonds. Bake for 10–15 minutes, until golden brown. Remove from oven and allow to cool.

Before serving, remove the pavlova nut-side down onto lightly sugared bakewell paper. Whip the cream to soft peaks, and reserving a quarter for decoration, spread the remainder over the meringue. Pick out a few of the best raspberries for decoration, and spread the remainder over the cream. To form the roulade, lift the bakewell paper from the back and roll carefully with the paper towards you. Slide the roulade off the paper and onto a suitable serving tray. Decorate with swirls of cream and the remaining raspberries. Keep cold until ready to serve.

Cuilmore Cottage

Raspberry Pecan Tart

created by
ANN NICOLL

We grow most of our own fruit and vegetables but we always have an absolute glut of raspberries; as they grow in such abundance in Scotland it is virtually impossible even to give them away! Over the years we, like many soft-fruit growers, have found it difficult to bring ourselves to eat them all, and even our children tend to avoid visiting us during the raspberry season!

I am always on the look-out for a lavish 'Mrs Beeton'-type recipe, 'Take 10 lb of raspberries . . .' In the meantime this recipe is very popular, although it uses far too few of the ubiquitous fruits!

Serves 4–6

for the base:

- 8 oz pecan nuts
- 3 tbsp sugar
- 8 oz plain flour
- 4 oz butter
- zest of 1 orange
- 1 egg

for the topping:

- 12 oz raspberries
- 12 oz white chocolate
- 4 oz double cream
- zest of 1 orange

Preheat oven to Gas 5/375°F/190°C.

Process all the ingredients for the base together until well mixed, then press into the bottom of an 11″ loose-bottomed cake tin. Bake for 20 minutes, and allow to cool.

Cover the base of the tart with the washed and picked raspberries, then melt together the chocolate, cream and orange zest. Pour this mixture over the raspberries, then chill the tart. Once set, decorate the top with chocolate flakes and whipped cream flavoured with Cointreau, plus a few more raspberries if you wish!

Cranachan

created by
JEFF BLAND

A traditional Scottish sweet, delicious served with a blackcurrant purée.

Serves 10

- 1½ pt double cream, whipped
- 4 oz sugar
- 5 oz mixed crushed shortbread and toasted Scottish pinhead oatmeal
- 4 oz soft berries (eg raspberries, strawberries, brambles or blackcurrants)
- 3 fl oz whisky
- 1 oz honey

Whip the double cream and sugar together, crush the shortbread and wash and drain the fruit. Add the whisky to the cream and fold in the shortbread and oatmeal, fruit and honey with a wooden spoon. When nicely mixed, put into a large bowl, or pipe into individual Paris goblets, and decorate or shape with spoons.

Raspberry Shortbread with a Passionfruit Coulis

created by
RUTH HADLEY

Good food comes from top-quality ingredients, and Scotland has some of the finest. 'Far better to buy good-quality mince than inferior steak.'

Serves 4

for the hazelnut biscuits:

4 oz butter
2 oz sugar
1 egg yolk
6 oz plain flour
4 oz hazelnuts, roasted and ground

for the passionfruit coulis:

6 passionfruit
2 fl oz fresh orange juice
½ lb fresh raspberries (the finest ones come from Blairgowrie)
icing sugar
1 oz sugar
¼ pt fresh double cream

To make the hazelnut biscuits, cream together the butter and sugar, add the egg yolk and flour, then lastly the hazelnuts. Make into a dough, then roll out carefully and cut into 3″ rounds. Place the rounds onto a greased baking tray, then CHILL for at least 30 minutes. Place in a pre-heated oven (Gas 5/375°F/190°C) and bake for 10–12 minutes, making sure they don't burn. Take out and leave to cool before carefully transferring into an air-tight container.

For the passionfruit coulis, cut each of the passionfruit in half and scoop out the flesh and seeds into a small pan. Add the orange juice and sugar, place on the heat and bring to a simmer, when the liquid will thicken slightly. Taste and add more sugar if you like (although it works better if it is slightly sharp). Place a sieve over a bowl and empty the contents of the pan into the sieve. Rub the sauce through the sieve to extract the seeds and then leave to cool.

Select the best half of the raspberries, and set aside for later. Put the remaining half in a food processor with a little icing sugar to taste. Whizz, then sieve to remove the seeds and reserve this sauce for later. Whip the double cream until it thickens.

To assemble the dessert, take four plates (if possible 8″ with a pretty border) and place one biscuit on each plate. Put a layer of whipped cream on the biscuit, then raspberries onto the whipped cream. Add a little more whipped cream and then 'bed' another biscuit on top, to form a sandwich. Surround the biscuit on the plate with the two fruit sauces. Finally, dust the top of the biscuit with a little icing sugar and garnish with three raspberries.

Any left-over biscuits can be saved in the air-tight container and are delicious served with ice cream.

Shortbread Biscuits Crowned by Seasonal Berries and Blackcurrant Meringue with Vanilla and Butterscotch Sauce

created by
JAMES HARDY

Serves 4

for the shortbread:
- 4½ oz plain flour
- 3 oz hard unsalted butter
- ½ oz icing sugar

for the meringue:
- 6 oz caster sugar
- 2 fl oz water
- 3 egg whites
- 1 fl oz blackcurrant juice

for the sauce:
- 4 egg yolks
- 3 oz sugar
- 1 vanilla pod, split lengthways
- ½ pt milk
- 1 fl oz blackcurrant juice
- 1½ oz butter
- 1½ oz soft brown sugar
- 1½ oz golden syrup
- 8 oz seasonal fruits (eg strawberries, raspberries, blueberries, blackcurrants)

Preheat oven to Gas 7/425°F/220°C.

To make the shortbread, blend the flour, butter and icing sugar in a mixer until bound together. Roll out the paste to ¼" (6mm) thickness and cut into rounds with a 3" (75mm) cutter. Bake for 5 minutes, then remove and leave to rest. Put the caster sugar and water in a copper pan and cook the sugar to 248°F/121°C. Meanwhile whisk the egg whites to form stiff peaks. Slowly pour the sugar syrup onto the whites, and beat until cold. Fold in 1 fl oz of blackcurrant juice.

For the sauce, cream the egg yolks and sugar in a bowl. In a saucepan bring the milk and vanilla pod to the boil. Pour the hot milk onto the yolks and sugar, then whisk in the butter, brown sugar and syrup and cook out to 225°F/105°C. Quickly cool over a bowl of ice.

Meanwhile, mix the berries with 1 fl oz of blackcurrant juice. Place a tablespoon of berries onto each biscuit, pipe meringue on top with a star nozzle, and bake for 4 minutes until browned. Arrange each biscuit in the centre of hot plates and border with the sauce. Garnish with a sprig of fresh mint and icing sugar.

Cromlix House

Lemon Tarte

created by
STEPHEN ROBERTSON

This marvellously rich and tangy tarte is an ideal end to any meal, formal or informal. Try serving it warm with summer berries or soft fruits and a raspberry sauce.

Serves 10

for the pastry:

8 oz plain flour
5 oz butter
3 oz caster sugar
1–2 eggs

for the filling:

9 eggs
8 oz caster sugar
zest of 2–3 lemons
juice of 5 lemons
250ml (½ pt) double cream

Preheat the oven to moderate.

Rub together the flour, butter and sugar until a crumb has formed, then incorporate the beaten eggs to bind the mixture. Roll out the pastry and use to line a greased 9″ flan dish. Bake blind in a moderate oven, and once you have removed the pastry shell turn the oven to low (Gas 4/350°F/180°C).

Meanwhile, whisk all the filling ingredients together. When the pastry shell is ready pour the filling in and bake for 20–30 minutes, until cooked through. Allow the tarte to cool slightly before cutting into portions.

The Vintners Rooms

Bramble and Almond Tart

created by

TIM CUMMING

If you have picked a surplus of brambles, make a bramble vinegar by steeping crushed brambles in a good white wine vinegar (1 lb : 1 pt) for 2–3 days. Strain and bottle. Excellent in a dressing for a wild mushroom salad etc.

Serves 6–8

for the sweet flan pastry:

- ½ lb plain flour
- 1½ oz ground almonds
- grated rind of ½ lemon
- 3 oz caster sugar
- pinch salt
- 6 oz butter
- 2 egg yolks
- 1 tbsp dark rum

for the batter:

- 5 tbsp double cream
- 2 whole eggs
- 4 tbsp vanilla sugar
- 3 tbsp ground almond
- 1 tbsp orange flower water
- 1 oz melted, cooled butter

for the filling:

- 1 lb brambles
- 1 fl oz Crème de Mures (or Cassis, or brandy)

Make the pastry in a food processor, blending the sifted flour, ground almonds, grated rind, sugar and salt. Add the cubed butter and egg yolks together with the rum, beaten together. Pulse and blend until just binding. Take out, form into a ball, and refrigerate for 30 minutes before use. Meanwhile, make the batter by simply whisking all the ingredients together.

To make the tart, line a 9–10″ flan dish with the sweet pastry, trimming off the surplus. Check over the brambles, and sprinkle the liqueur or brandy over. Fill the flan with the brambles, pour over the batter, and bake in a hot oven (Gas 7/425°F/220°C) for 20–30 minutes (until the batter is just set). Serve hot with double cream.

Caledonian Ice Cream

created by

ELAINE M KNOX

'The Chip', as it is affectionately known, was described as 'a legend in its own lunchtime' by the judges who named it Macallan/Decanter Scottish Restaurant of the Year in 1991, and the plaudits continue, with the title of Egon Ronay Scottish Cellar of the Year 1993 and International Wine Challenge Scottish Wine Merchant of the Year, 1994/5.

for the caramelized oatmeal:

- 3 oz (75g) caster sugar
- 4 tbsp water
- 2 oz (50g) pinhead oatmeal

for the ice cream:

- 1 pt (570 ml) whipping cream
- ½ tsp pure vanilla extract

for the syrup:

- 4 oz (110g) caster sugar
- 4 tbsp water

Start off by making the caramelized oatmeal. Put the caster sugar and water in a small saucepan over a low heat and leave for 5 minutes. Then take a medium-sized frying pan, place it on a medium heat, and when the pan is hot add the oatmeal and swirl it around the pan constantly so that it browns evenly, which it will do in about 5 minutes. Remove the oatmeal to a plate to prevent it becoming over-brown. By now the sugar in the saucepan will have dissolved, so you can turn the heat right up and let it boil (watching it like a hawk) until it begins to turn a rich caramel colour, rather like dark runny honey.

As soon as it reaches that stage, stir in the toasted oatmeal, remove from the heat and quickly pour the mixture over the oiled baking sheet, then leave it on one side to get cold and firm (approximately 15 minutes). Now take off small pieces at a time and pound them in a pestle and mortar until the mixture resembles something the size of salt crystals. Place these in a bowl and keep covered until you are ready to make the ice cream.

To make the sugar syrup, measure the sugar and water into a small saucepan, place over a gentle heat and stir until the sugar has dissolved—about 5 minutes. Then remove from the heat and allow to cool completely.

Now to make the ice cream: pour the cold syrup into a mixing bowl along with the whipping cream, add the vanilla, and whisk with an electric hand-whisk until the mixture just begins to thicken and hold its shape. Then pour this mixture into an ice-cream maker and freeze-churn until it is firm but still pliable—this will take about 30–40 minutes. Now transfer it to a bowl and fold in the oatmeal mixture evenly, then spoon it into the tin, cover with a double thickness of foil, and freeze until needed.

To serve, remove from the freezer to the refrigerator about 20 minutes before required. Then dip the base and side of the tin in hot water for 10 seconds or so, loosen all round the edges with a palette knife, then turn it on to a plate. Using a sharp knife dipped in hot water, cut the ice cream into slices and serve on large plates with either soft fruits or a fruit compote or coulis.

Dryburgh Abbey Hotel

Chocolate, Liqueur and Pear Cream

created by
PATRICK RUSE

A wickedly rich, dark and alcoholic dessert.

Serves 4

2 pears
¼ pint port
4 oz broken bitter chocolate
4 eggs, separated
2 fl oz Grand Marnier
2 fl oz brandy
4 fl oz double cream, whipped
pinch sea salt

Skin and core the pears, then cut into quarters lengthways. Poach in the port for 5 minutes and allow to cool. Meanwhile place the broken chocolate in a bowl set over a pan of water over the heat until it melts. Put the egg yolks into another bowl and pour the melted chocolate over them, stirring to blend the mixture well. To this mixture add the liqueurs and cream, and mix together thoroughly. Beat the egg whites with a pinch of salt, and fold them into the chocolate cream carefully so that the mixture is fully blended but still light and fluffy. Remove the pears from the port, cut into small cubes and arrange in ramekin dishes. Spoon the chocolate mixture on top of the pears and chill for 2 hours before serving.

Gateau Truffle au Chocolat

created by
NEIL ROSS

Serve this luxuriously rich truffle cake in a pool of delicate orange and pistachio sauce.

Serves 10 generously

for the chocolate Genoese sponge:

4 eggs
4 oz caster sugar
3 oz flour
1 oz cocoa powder
2 oz butter

for the gateau truffle:

13 oz dark bitter couverture or milk chocolate
13 oz double cream
4 tbsp Tia Maria
2 tbsp cognac

for the orange and pistachio sauce:

1 pt milk
zest of 1 large orange
4 oz pistachio nuts, finely chopped
6 egg yolks
3 oz caster sugar

To make the sponge, whisk the eggs and sugar with a balloon whisk in a bowl over a pan of hot water. Continue until the mixture is slightly creamy and doubled in bulk. At this point, remove from the heat and whisk until cold and thick, at the ribbon stage. Now fold in the flour and cocoa powder, very gently, and add the melted butter. Place in a greased, floured 8″ Genoese mould and bake in a moderately hot oven (Gas 7/ 425°F/220°C) for about 20 minutes.

Meanwhile prepare the truffle mixture. Roughly chop the couverture and melt in a bowl over a pan of hot water, being careful not to overheat. Allow to cool, but not solidify. Whisk the double cream with the Tia Maria until it reaches the light ribbon stage then place in the refrigerator to keep cool.

Place the chocolate Genoese sponge into an 8″ flan ring and brush with the brandy. Refrigerate for 10 minutes. Once the chocolate has cooled, fold in half of the whipped cream to half of the chocolate and whisk well. Then add the rest of the melted chocolate and cream and fold in lightly. Do not over work the mixture.

Pour the truffle mixture into the chilled Genoese sponge flan ring, using a palate knife to push it outwards from the centre to the edges of the ring. Smooth the top with the palate knife. Chill for 2–3 hours, until the truffle mixture has set.

To make the orange and pistachio sauce, place the milk in a saucepan and heat slowly. Add the grated orange zest and pistachio nuts. Place the egg yolks and caster sugar into a bowl and whisk. Pour in the milk and other ingredients and whisk. Return the mixture to the saucepan and cook slowly for about 5 minutes. Allow to cool, and when cold serve with the chocolate truffle cake.

Clafoutis of Apples, Drambuie Ice Cream and Raspberry Coulis

created by
PAUL WHITECROSS

Clafoutis is a traditional butter cake, and despite the French name the Scottish ingredients stand out well in this honest, simple and flavoursome dish. Assembling the dessert can obviously be made easier, for example if you don't have an ice-cream maker or simply do not have time, a good quality vanilla ice cream will do. If you feel a little more adventurous, whisk your ice cream until slightly soft, add the Drambuie, mix, and return to the freezer.

Serves 4

for the Drambuie ice cream (makes enough for 10):

1 pt milk
1 vanilla pod
6 egg yolks
3 oz sugar
4 fl oz double cream
3 fl oz Drambuie

for the raspberry coulis (makes enough for 10):

¼ pt water
11 oz caster sugar
1½ lb raspberries
4 fl oz framboise liqueur

for the clafoutis:

4 eggs
5 oz sugar
9 oz flour
½ pt double cream
3 apples, peeled and finely sliced

to garnish:

20 raspberries
20 redcurrant sprigs
4 sprigs mint

First make the Drambuie ice cream. In a medium saucepan bring the milk, with the vanilla pod split into it, to the boil.

Whisk together the egg yolk and sugar in a bowl until pale, then pour on the milk, a little at a time, whisking continuously. Return the mixture to another saucepan and cook over a medium heat, stirring with a wooden spoon. As the custard starts to thicken, ie when it begins to coat the back of a spoon, pour through a sieve to remove the vanilla pod and allow to cool in a plastic container. When cool, add the Drambuie and place in an ice-cream maker, and as it starts to solidify add the cream and continue to churn. Remove when ready and store in a plastic airtight container.

Meanwhile make the raspberry coulis. Make a sugar syrup by bringing the water and sugar to the boil. Remove from the heat and while still hot add the raspberries. Allow to cool and infuse for an hour, then blend well in a blender. Strain through a fine sieve into a plastic container or bowl to remove any seeds then add framboise liqueur.

For the clafoutis, whisk together the eggs and sugar until they are frothy. Gradually mix in the flour then add the cream and whisk until the mixture has at least doubled in size. Allow the mix to rest for about 30 minutes in a refrigerator. Lightly oil an ovenproof dish (enough for 4 people or 4 individual moulds) and place the finely sliced apple in the mould in a clockwise direction. Pour over the batter and cook in a preheated oven (Gas 4/350°F/180°C) for about 15 minutes or until set.

To assemble the dessert, spoon the raspberry coulis into the centre of four plates. Place the clafoutis in the middle of the coulis, top with a scoop of Drambuie ice cream, and garnish with a sprig of mint and some raspberries and redcurrants dusted with icing sugar.

Beremeal Bannocks

created by

ALAN CRAIGIE

Beremeal, or bearmeal, is a rare form of Scottish barley worth hunting out to make this traditional recipe.

- 4 oz plain flour
- 1 tsp salt
- 1 heaped tsp cream of tartar
- 2 heaped tsp baking soda
- 12 oz beremeal
- 2 oz butter
- 1 pt buttermilk

Sieve the flour, salt, soda and tartar together and add the beremeal. Rub in the butter to give a crumb, then mix in enough buttermilk to give a soft dough. Form into bannocks and cook on a hot girdle 2–3 minutes each side, until golden brown.

Glossary of Culinary Terms

bain-marie a tin or other vessel of hot water into which another container, holding food, is placed to cook the food gently or keep it warm.

bake blind to cook an empty pastry shell so that it remains crisp when a creamy or liquid filling is added. Line the flan tin with pastry then place a piece of greaseproof paper or tin foil over the bottom, cover with dry beans, and bake in a moderately hot oven for approximately 12 minutes. Remove the beans and paper, and return to the oven for a further 5 minutes or until golden brown.

cartouche a circle of buttered greaseproof paper, cut to fit the circumference of a pan and placed over it to protect the food during cooking.

concasse food prepared by fine chopping, most commonly skinned deseeded tomato flesh.

coulis a thin purée, usually of fruit but occasionally of vegetables, fish or fowl.

couverture a type of chocolate containing a higher than usual proportion of fat, with a low melting point, used mainly for coating and covering.

dariole a small round mould, usually used for preparing pastry shells.

deglaze to dilute the juices etc left in a pan by the addition of liquid, most commonly wine.

julienne thin strips, usually of vegetables, often deep fried or cooked lightly in butter, or used raw for garnish.

jus juice, usually from meat, or gravy.

mirepoix a selection of vegetables finely diced and sautéed, often used as a base for sauces (named after the Duc de Lévis-Mirepoix, an 18th-century French general, whose chef invented the dish).

mousseline a light mousse made with whipped cream.

nappe to coat food with a smooth sauce, from French *nappe*, tablecloth.

roux a mixture of melted butter and flour in equal parts, cooked lightly or browned depending on the sauce, used to thicken many types of sauce.

suprême breast and wing of chicken (or game), or a fine fillet of fish. To prepare a suprême of chicken, remove and set aside the leg then separate the flesh on both sides of the breastbone by cutting down towards the wing joints. Pull the joints of the wings away from the bird, keeping them attached to the breast, and finally cut through each wing at the second joint to remove the tip, or pinion. Ease the skin off carefully.

terrine a deep, straight-sided dish with a tightly fitted lid, or a preparation cooked and pressed in such a dish, often served in slices. A loaf tin can be substituted in many recipes.

Index

Notes

Notes

Notes

Notes

Notes

Notes

Notes

Notes

Notes